"Fruit that Will Last"
Copyright © 1999 by Tim Hawkins
Third Impression 2004

Requests for information should be addressed to:
Youth Ministry, PO Box 1226
Castle Hill. N.S.W. 1765, Australia
E-mail: crossfire@stpaulscastlehill.org.au
Website: www.crossfireyouth.com.au

UK Distribution by
The Good Book Company
Elm House, 37 Elm Road
New Malden, Surrey KT3 3HB
Tel: 0845-225-0880; Fax: 0845-225-0990
email: admin@thegoodbook.co.uk
www.thegoodbook.co.uk

ISBN: 0-646-37605-5

Published by Hawkins Ministry Resources.
Printed in Hong Kong

"May I recommend ..."

"I have been waiting for Tim to write this book for ten years. He is Australia's best kept secret when it comes to building a youth ministry for a lasting impact.

The average youth pastor in our nation lasts for 18 months. Tim has served God as a youth pastor for over 20 years raising up many disciples of Jesus Christ. I totally commend Tim Hawkins to you and know that you will gain from his wisdom, experience and insight to youth ministry. Tim has validated youth ministry in its own right, and by serving young people for over two decades has clearly shown that it is not "just a stepping stone to the real ministry".

I encourage every youth leader to read this book and use it as a manual to build and resource your youth ministry."

Christine Caine
NSW Director
Youth Alive

" ... Tim is a man of passion and ability ... He has a passion to tell people about Jesus and a passion to make young people disciples of Jesus. Tim has exercised this ministry with great persistence, thoughtfulness and success. The outcome has been many many young people's lives changed, disciples made and youth leaders and workers produced. His ministry has been very significant.

The significance of his ministry has derived, among other things, from two great abilities. He is an excellent communicator. Tim thinks out what he wants to say, illustrates it well and states it clearly. You cannot but listen to him He is also a strategic thinker. Tim's moves are unhurried and always purposeful. He works very hard at making every move effect. The long term result is that his influence is widespread for the Kingdom".

Reg Piper
Anglican Bishop of Wollongong

Other resources by Tim Hawkins:

The **"Growing Young Disciples"** Series is a 5 book series aimed at helping junior highs become passionate disciples of Jesus. These 5 bible study books contain the essential foundations for producing "fruit that will last", and they are the leading disciple-making materials in Australia for junior highs.

This series is published by Christian Education Publications, PO Box A287 Sydney NSW 2000 Australia

Book 1	Discovering Jesus
Book 2	First Steps
Book 3	Second Thoughts
Book 4	Life to the Max
Book 5	How to really Stick At Being a Christian

"The Heartbeat of Youth Ministry"

This 8 cassette series is a complete youth ministry conference in itself. Tim delivers 8 dynamic messages to inspire you to build long-term disciples in your youth ministry.

"Ultimate Victory"

This 8 cassette series unfolds the ultimate victory of Jesus from the Book of Revelation. Tim shows high-schoolers how they can experience this victory in their life as he illustrates this final book in the bible in a down-to-earth way.

"Awesome on the Inside"

This 5 cassette series challenges high school disciples to be re-made by God "from the inside". Tim shows from the bible how Gods Spirit can rebuild your heart to make the you the man or woman that God has designed you to be.

All cassette series are available from the addresses on Page ii.

Thanks heaps ...

To Jesus Christ.   Without you, not only would there be no book, but I would have no life. You have taken me to The Father, and filled me with your Spirit. Without you, I can do nothing.

To my wife, Karen. It was your encouragement that started me writing this book, and I deeply appreciate the way you put up with me as I finished it. I love you!

To Walter Crutchfield. You have impacted my thinking about youth ministry more than anyone I know. Each time I meet you I see things in a clearer, more biblical light. Much of the material in this book stems from your ideas and inspiration .

To Doug Fields. I loved catching up with you at Saddleback, and you clarified my thinking in so many ways. You are the inspiration being the discipleship HABITS that we use, and your book "Purpose Driven Youth Ministry" is fantastic.

To Bo Boshers.   You were such a deep encouragement to me when I caught up with you at Willow Creek. What you have sown into me is being reproduced throughout Australia.   Your book (with Kim Anderson) "Student Ministry for the 21st Century" is a "must have"!

To Tommy Gilmore. Your simple "3 step strategy" for making disciples has been inspirational for our work here. Thank you for sharing your thoughts with me.

To Eric Liechty. Much of our "No Regrets" Year 12 ministry originated with your excellent thoughts and ideas. Thanks heaps!

To Rick Bond, Rod Story and "Evangelism Explosion" Gang. You have given us the tools to make our students personally evangelistic. The strategy and illustrations from Evangelism Explosion pervade our ministry.

To Chris Dredge. You did the "hack work" to make this book a possibility. You encouraged me just when I needed it. Thank you for the cover design, and thank you **Nathan Drabsch** for your great artwork. Thank you **Stuart Larkin,** my daughter **Carly**, and my sister **Karen** for your superb proof reading and final editing.

To the students and leaders at "Crossfire" in sunny downtown Castle Hill. Thank you for allowing me to take you on the exciting journey of having your life turned around by Jesus. I love hanging out with you guys and I know God will use you to impact this world.

I have taken great care to give due credit to the number of individuals who have impacted my life and ministry. After two decades in ministry, it is possible that I have inadvertently included material which has not been properly acknowledged. If this has happened, please contact the publisher so that this can be rectified in future editions.

Contents

Section Seven - Appendix

How to Grow Fruit That Will Last

SECTION 1

Chapter 1
The One Question I Forgot to Ask

1. The First Day

"Here is our new Youth Pastor!" I stepped forward at my new church to thunderous applause. There were high-schoolers all over the place. Excited that I was there. But their enthusiasm was nothing compared with how good I was feeling.

"This is it!" I told myself. "No longer am I merely some small group leader in the back-blocks of junior high ministry. I have made it!"

Years of study (well ... not that many years .. and come to think of it ... not that much study!) had prepared me for this moment. I WAS THE NEW YOUTH PASTOR. Head honcho. In charge. King of the kids. A new direction in youth ministry.

I had dreamed about this. I had pictured sitting down in the gutter with some street kid who would see the error of his ways and discover Christ in a radical conversion. I imagined the busloads of teenagers who would come to the stadium because I was going to speak. All the "old ways" of youth ministry were gone. I was here. Yes, humble, Christlike, a servant of all, but I was going to make a success of it where others had failed. All the boring bits of youth ministry were gone. I was going to launch a dynamic thunderbolt which would shatter the stereotypes and move Christian Youth Ministry into the world of tomorrow.

Not for my own glory, of course. I truly wanted to serve Christ. As long as they got my name right on the programme.

2. 21 years later

I cannot believe how self-centred I was then. Twenty one years later I can look back with amazement that God has kept me in youth ministry for this long. All my colleagues seem to have fallen by the wayside. Those young ambitious youth pastors that started out with me all seem to be doing other things. Some have gone back to "real jobs" (you know, the sort that pay "real money"!) Some have moved onto "real ministry" (they're now "real" pastors in "real" churches). Many, sadly, have left ministry all together. Some have walked away from Christ all together.

God has left me here. Why? Maybe he won't let me leave youth ministry until I get it right! (Do you get the suspicion that I'm a slow learner?) God has taught me so much over the 21 years that I have been a youth pastor of a local church. This book reflects 21 years of learning - and I'm really keen as to what the next 21 years will bring. If only someone had told me all this stuff 21 years ago! But then again, I'm not sure I would have listened!

3. The one question we all want to ask

Whenever youth pastors and youth leaders get together, there's always one question that you're dying to ask. Some of you are brazen enough to come right out and ask it; others of us are reserved and shy and only dream about asking it. But for every youth leader this is a burning question you want to ask any youth leader from another church - and you really want to know the answer.

Here it is - in blazing black and white. The question that bugs us all.

"How many kids in your youth group?"

There! I've said it! But be honest. You really want to know, don't you? And you're desperately hoping that they will give you a number that is a **little less** than the number that come to **your** youth group.

True?

When your fellow youth leader from another church gives you an answer to your question, you'd really like to be able to answer *"Oh! That's a great number! You should be very encouraged! I can remember when our group only had that many"*

Ouch! It's not that all us youth leaders are megalomaniacs. Deep down, being better than the other guy is not what drives us. Nearly every youth pastor I meet has a genuine desire to serve Jesus. An honest passion to build young disciples. A genuine drive to make a difference in the lives of students. And it is this desire, this passion, this drive that steers us towards asking dumb questions like *"How many kids in your youth group?"* **because we desperately want to know that we're going okay.**

4. The stakes are high

Why are you in youth ministry? For most of you, you genuinely love Jesus, and you genuinely love students, and you want to be able to bring the two of them together. You know it really matters. Depending on which survey you read, up to 85% of people who will become Christians in their life will do so before their 18th birthday. Youth ministry is vitally important. That's why you're doing it! That's why you went to the conference. That's why you're reading the book.

Because you really care about what you're doing, you need to know that you're going okay. And we all work out that the dude with the biggest youth ministry must be doing okay. Right?

Well, I want you to relax. Take a deep breath. Soak in the next sentence. Ready?

5. God doesn't care how many kids are in your youth group.

Read it again. **God doesn't care how many kids are in your youth group.**

Heh?

Imagine that you are no longer a youth leader, but you are a fruit grower. You own an orchard, and you grow fruit. Around you there are lots of other fruit growers. They all have orchards, and they all grow fruit. Some have big orchards, some have small orchards. But you all grow fruit.

How do you work out whether you are doing your job well? How do you know if you are a good fruit grower? If there is a local fair, where there is a "Best Fruit Grower" award, how will the judges determine who wins?

No-one gives a rat's armpit as to how many trees you have in your orchard! Here is the important question **"What sort of fruit are you producing?"** What is the quality of your fruit? Is it good fruit? And more importantly - **Will it last?** No-one wants fruit that will "go off" after a few days.

The farmer who's got 300 fruit trees in his orchard -but produces low-quality fruit that "goes off" a few days after picking - that's not the place where you'll go and buy your fruit! He will never win any award! But the farmer who only has 100 fruit trees but produces large quantities of good quality fruit that lasts for weeks ... there's your prize winner! That's the place to go shopping! That's where you get fruit that really satisfies!

Can you see the number of fruit trees in the orchard makes not one scrap of difference as to how good the fruit-grower is? It is the quality of the fruit. Yes, numbers do make a difference, but what if the farmer with 100 trees is producing more fruit that than the farmer with 300 trees? An orchard with fruitless trees is of no use to anyone!

6. God cares incredibly about the quality of your fruit

Just before he died, Jesus instructed his followers about the lives they were to lead, and the ministry they were to have.

He says in **John 15:16**

> *"You did not choose me, but I chose you and appointed you to go and bear fruit - fruit that will last"*

Are you special, or what? Jesus has chosen you and appointed you for the specific purpose that you will bear fruit. And not just any fruit. Not poor quality fruit. Not fruit that will "go off " after a day or so. Jesus has chosen you so that you will bear **fruit that will last.**

7. The one question which I forgot to ask

The one question which I forgot to ask those 21 years ago.

"Am I producing fruit that will last?"

Now we could get all long and involved about what this "fruit" really means, but lets keep this simple. It certainly includes the "fruit" of your personal life, and it certainly includes the "fruit" of your ministry. We'll get stuck into these in later sections.

But to get your creative juices flowing, have a look at the next 2 chapters.

Chapter 2
Will Your Fruit Survive Long Term?

1. Our Instant World

"What do we want?" (insert your favourite cause)
"When do we want it? NOW"

I love living at the turn of the millennium. Everything is so instant. I can push a button and have the world on my TV screen NOW. I can start the microwave and have a cup of coffee NOW. I can tap into the internet and have the world's knowledge at my fingertips NOW.

I love it! We have a day/night medical centre where I can just walk in and see a doctor inside 15 minutes. I can video my kids and watch it straight away on the TV. I can reach for the phone and dial up a pizza. We built a new house and inside one day the yard was completely turfed and a magnificent garden planted. In one day! I love it!

2. We All Want Instant Results

Everyone offers instant results. "Lose 10 kilograms in 10 weeks" (I'm going to do that one day). "Double your investments overnight" "10 steps to being a person of influence". "Take this tablet and your pain will go away" Sometimes we believe that if we can't see the results immediately, then it's not worth doing.

But ask anyone who has raised a child. There are no instant results. It is a lifetime investment. Ask anyone who has won Olympic Gold. It doesn't happen overnight. It is years of strain and pain. Ask anyone who has graduated from university. There were many sleepless nights of relentless study. The things that are really worth achieving are usually a long-term investment.

3. The problem of 'Instant Youth Ministry'

When most people think "Youth Ministry", they're thinking "Instant results".

Here's the way it often works. Pastor Bloggs ministers at a small but solid church. Many of his church members have children, who are now growing into teenagers.

"We ought to do something for the young people" Mrs Battersby mumbles one day. *"Church is fine for me, but my high-schoolers won't come near the place. Why can't we do something for the youth of the area?"*

The grumbling continues until the Rev Bloggs realises he has a problem on this hands.

He knows 2 things for sure.
1. He's gotta do something about "those young people"
2. He himself doesn't want anything to do with "those young people"

Solution? Get a youth pastor! Full time, part time, trained, untrained ... it doesn't matter, as long as **someone** does something about those young people.

The youth pastor is appointed. There's only one catch. There's only enough money to employ someone for one year. *"No guarantee that there'll be any funds for next year"* our bold new recruit is told. *"That will all depend on what results you get this year"*

The scene is now set for another youth ministry disaster. Instant results are required to keep the whole thing going. This is a recipe for a church that will be disappointed; a youth pastor who will quit the ministry, and students who will have an initial excitement, but then drift away, never to be seen again, and awfully suspicious of the **next** youth pastor that the hapless Rev Bloggs is obliged to employ.

4. The pressure inside us

Even if there is no pressure from the outside, many of us youth pastors and youth leaders feel the need for instant results. We want to feel that we're going well. We want to see some results for all our hard work. We want to feel accepted and needed. We want to make our mark on the world. If there was a book called "You Can Revolutionise Your Youth Ministry and Double Your Numbers in 12 Weeks", we would buy it.

So we go for the quickest results that we can imagine. Numbers. "If only I could get the worlds loudest rock group" "If only we could offer better entertainment" "If only we could blow up the stage"

The problem with all this is simply "Where are you looking?" We're wanting to see fast growth. So we bring our "plants" into a hothouse to accelerate things. We jazz up the activities. We buy a smoke machine. Double the PA. Tell lots of emotional stories that will get kids crying.

But the test of a hothouse is not how well the plants grow while they're there. The test of a hothouse is whether it prepares the plants for robust and solid growth **once they have left the protected environment of the hothouse.** If you keep your eye on the future result, you will have a ministry that is right for the present.

5. The test for your youth ministry

Here is the question you must ask yourself about the effectiveness of your youth ministry.

Will your students stand firmly for Christ long after they have left the protective environment of your youth ministry?

We're not in the business of running successful youth groups. We're not called by Jesus to build large numbers that will impress people. We are called by Christ to produce "fruit that will last".

Those junior highs that got all excited at the last camp that you ran - will they be standing strong for Christ in 5 years -10 years - 25 years time?

Those high-schoolers who kept coming to those "Pizza Pig-Outs" that you ran each month - will they be actively living for Christ and ministering for Christ in their adult life? When your vibrant youth group is only but a distant memory, will the students who came under your influence in their teenage years be the ministry leaders and church planters of the coming decades?

In short, **will your fruit survive and grow outside the hothouse?**

Quick answer: If it's only the excitement and hype of your youth ministry that is keeping them going, they will probably wither and die outside the hothouse. But if you are sowing God's Word and God's Love into young lives - building disciples for the long-term -with your eyes **not on the hothouse of your youth ministry, but on the reality of their future adult life,** then you have every chance of fulfilling Jesus' command to bear "fruit that will last". More about all this in the coming chapters!

6. 'Fruit that will last' - what does it look like?

One of our problems is that youth pastors and youth leaders do not stay in youth ministry long enough to bring about these long term results. Go to a Youth Pastors Conference and try to find someone who's been a youth pastor for longer than 5 years. Or one who has been at his current church for longer than 3 years!

But if you keep your eye on the future .. and prepare your "plants" for a lifetime of ministry "outside the hothouse" ... here is what "fruit that will last" might look like.

> **Roland** * was in Year 12 at High School when I arrived as youth pastor. I met him on our week-long camp. He was the one who delighted in parading in his underwear late at night past the girls cabins. If there was a smart-alec answer, it was usually Roland behind it. The year after High School he went overseas as an exchange student, and progressively set about breaking every commandment that God had ever ordained.

But he had been discipled well in his teenage years, and through prayer and much anguish, he came back to Jesus. I took him under my wing and trained him for ministry. I took him back to his old high school to minister to students. He learned about living for Christ and ministering for Christ. I helped train him as a disciple over a number of years. He helped oversee a large section of our youth ministry. He is now an Associate Pastor in a church on the other side of town. He is heading up a ministry that I believe will impact our whole nation.

This was a group effort by many of us. It is "fruit that will last"

Sam * is typical of many of our students. Brought along to our youth groups by his parents, he was challenged by one of the adults in our church to be "fair dinkum" about his faith, and in Year 8 he joined a "Discovering Jesus" group with a small bunch of other Year 8 blokes. I had the privilege of helping to disciple him in this small group throughout his high-school life. It was hugely encouraging to see him make a stand for Jesus against his non-believing teachers at his State High School It was a joy to see him elected as school captain and to publicly proclaim Christ from that position. He has now married a Christian girl, moved out of the area, and is faithfully ministering at another church, ready to raise a household of faith.

Fruit that will last.

7. A warning

Not everyone is a "success" story. Our ministry is littered with kids who gave up on church, dropped out of life, walked away from Jesus. There are no guarantees. Every person must make his own decisions and stand accountable before Jesus for that. The challenge of discipleship is not one that every student wants to take on. The demands of Christlike growth are not what every parent wants from our youth ministry.

This book is not about "recipes for success" It is more about "planning for faithfulness". Let us raise up a generation of young people who are ready for a lifetime of active ministry. Let's impact this planet by faithfully discipling those students whom God has placed before us.

It is God who gives the growth.

I Corinthians 3:6

"I planted the seed, Apollos watered it, but God gave the growth"

Let's see if we can learn how to be faithful planters and waterers, so with God's blessing of growth, we will indeed produce "fruit that will last".

But just before we learn how to do that, let me warn you about 5 enemies that will stand in your way.

Chapter 3
5 Cheap Substitutes for Quality Fruit

Why do so many youth ministries fail to produce "fruit that will last?" It's not because we don't want to. I believe that there are thousands upon thousands of youth pastors and youth leaders who desperately, passionately want to see this world won for Christ. There is no lack of enthusiasm. The problem is - there are 5 cheap substitutes for quality fruit that will delight you and seduce you, and take you away from the mission that Jesus has designed for you.

Your master, Jesus, has sent you out to acquire "fruit that will last". On your shopping trip, there are many temptations and specials designed to distract you from your faithful, reliable shopping list.

An informed shopper is a wise shopper. So watch out for these shonky deals and cheap substitutes.

Cheap substitute No. 1. Numbers

No matter how many times you hear this said, this cheap substitute **always** has the power to distract you from what Jesus has called you to achieve.

a) There's Nothing Wrong with Numbers

Let's say at the outset, there is nothing wrong with numbers. I mean, there's a whole book of the bible named after them! People matter to God, and people can be counted. Good ministries often have large numbers. Being at one of the larger churches in Australia, I sometimes get the feeling from pastors at other (smaller) churches, that if you're getting good numbers, it is sure proof that you must be doing something wrong!

No, large numbers are not necessarily evil, and yet they are not necessarily good. Larger numbers simply give you a greater potential to do more good-or more harm!

> I remember when I was learning to drive. I learned on a little 4 cylinder 1200cc engine car. All my mistakes were little ones. The engine was not very powerful. Then I had a friend let me practice on his V8 Charger. Whoa! All my little mistakes suddenly became BIG mistakes, and I was a learner-driver out of control.

Large numbers are like that. They enable you to have a larger impact on this world - for good - or for evil. They can be a tremendous tool in having very effective ministry. And yet, numbers are an alluring seducer.

b) Everyone wants numbers

There is huge pressure to attract big numbers in your youth ministry. The senior pastor wants big numbers because he wants to attract many families to his church; the board of elders or deacons want big numbers so they can include them in their annual reports; parents want big numbers so there will be an attractive youth group that little Johnny will want to attend; the students themselves like big numbers cos they want to belong to something that looks successful ... and ... well, YOU want big numbers, don't you? I mean, you don't want to run some small, insignificant show, do you? You want to make an impact - a BIG impact - and think of all those lives you can win for Christ! And of course, the bigger the numbers, the more important you will feel, and the more respect everyone else will give you (not that you would think of these things, of course!)

c) The Danger of Numbers

Here is the subtle seduction of numbers: it's when they **take over** as your main aim. Hey! Any idiot can attract large numbers! Even senior pastors can attract large crowds! Hitler attracted the multitudes! If all you are after is large numbers at your youth ministry, then offer free beer!

The problem with numbers is that we can lose sight of our goals to make disciples simply to keep the numbers up. There is the danger of watering down the gospel, softening the message, or changing our focus to "keep the kids coming". I even knew of a church that had a monthly "outreach" event - where the Christian students were encouraged to invite their non-Christian friends, and so that they wouldn't be embarrassed to invite their friends, they were guaranteed that "the gospel would not be mentioned"

Aarrgghh! Do you see the problem? To attract numbers, they had just given up the one impactful message from God which is *"the power to save all who believe" (**Romans 1: 16-17**)*

d) The re-birth of Crossfire

When I arrived here at St Paul's we had a vibrant youth ministry going. That is, vibrant in the sense that there were hundreds of teenagers here, and for many years, many faithful leaders had been seeking to get alongside them and bring them to Christ. But here was the trap. To keep the lines of communication open, our leadership team had to put hours and hours of effort in to come up with attractive activities so that the youth of the district would want to come along to our turf. Our youth groups were wild - crazy - full of life -and bursting at the seams.

But here's what I noticed. Despite the apparent "success" of these nights, we were not building disciples. We were building attenders. 80% of our leaders' effort was put into getting kids to come along and be entertained. We simply didn't have the energy or time to put consistent work into those students who were responding. The students came to have "fun" - while we were (allegedly) running the group to bring students to Christ. There was an obvious conflict.

I challenged our leadership team with these stark realities; we had stacks of trees in the orchard, but very little fruit. In prayer, and with great caution, we made a dramatic change. We were going to put 80% of our effort into bringing students to Christ, and only a small amount into making our group attractive in other ways. That is, we wanted the **gospel** to be the attraction of our group. We made our preaching central - and challenged students to respond.

That is, we decided to target the *already interested* rather than the *not interested at all*.

Result No 1

Inside 6 months we halved our numbers. Halved. 50% cut back. Divided by two. We went from 320 per Friday to 160 per Friday. Ouch!

Result No 2

We doubled our fruit. That is, we had more students come to Christ and grow as disciples than we had had in any other year. By making the gospel central, we stopped focussing on numbers (cheap substitute) and started focussing on fruit (the real thing).

PS No 1: Our numbers have since risen, and are starting to get back to the level that they were before the change. But this time we're doing it with the gospel as the focus. We're after fruit that will last, not the cheap substitute.

PS No 2: If you want to know **how** we made that change, the rest of this book will explain what God has taught us!

Cheap Substitute No. 2 - Activities

a) The "Let's Take them Out" strategy

Let me tell you how nearly every new youth group starts.

"Let's make this better than the old youth group"
"How do we do that?"
"Let's ask the kids what they want to do"
"Okay kids - what do you want to do?"
LET'S GO BOWLING / SKATING / TIMEZONE / MOVIES / BEACH / GO KARTING etc. etc

Nothing wrong with all these wholesome activities.

Maybe you even do one of these in your youth group from time to time.

But I know of groups which **centre** their programme around outings and activities. You know, like every second week.

Simply ask the question. "Will it help us make disciples"

And don't be fooled. The students who are keen to come water-sliding with you, won't necessarily be keen to study the bible with you.

> I can remember when Darren was in Year 10 at high school. He was in a discipleship group that I led, and was growing strongly as a man in Christ. He had a younger brother who attended a youth group at a church down the road.

> "At my brother's youth group", he said to me thoughtfully one day "they have an outing every second week". I could tell by the tone in his voice that he was suggesting "why can't we do that too?"

> I asked Darren "Do you think that those outings are helping your brother to become a disciple?". He thought for a moment. "No -I guess they're not". The point was made.

> Darren is now one of my most trusted leaders in our youth ministry. His younger brother is a long way from Christ.

Nothing wrong with the odd outing (although we don't have them at Crossfire). But if they become your focus, it is a cheap substitute for building fruit that will last.

b) The "Let's keep them busy" strategy

This is the "Christian" version of substituting activities for real discipleship.

See if any of these sound familiar

> *"At our church we run activities 7 nights a week for our young people. We have choir on Monday nights; basketball on Tuesday nights; bible study on Wednesday nights; working bee on Thursday nights; Youth Group on Friday Nights; Social outings on Saturday Nights; and Church on Sunday Nights. It keeps them out of trouble!"*

> *"We gotta keep running our youth group during the holidays - otherwise our kids would all go down to the pub"*

> *"We gotta run a big camp after the HSC - otherwise all our Year 12s would go on schoolies week"*

Does this sound to you like a ministry that is "bearing fruit that will last"? Trained disciples don't need endless activities to keep them out of mischief. A trained disciple will learn how to use their leisure time in a Christlike way. A trained disciple will be able to deal with "schoolies week". If the only thing that is keeping your students out of mischief is the activities that you run, then you are not building "fruit that will last". As soon as they move out of your "activities empire", they will be "fruit that goes off".

Activities can be a cheap substitute for "fruit that will last"

Cheap Substitute No. 3. - Hype

"Hype" happens at every youth activity. You don't want a dull, boring, lifeless programme. You will want to have an excited crowd, motivated students, "the best you can do".

I believe youth ministries have a lot to teach the rest of the Christian Church in this area. For too long, many of our church services and other programmes have been marked by mediocrity and boredom. I once heard it said that "if anyone gets converted in an Anglican church service, then we know it **has** to be the Holy Spirit! There's nothing about the church service that could even vaguely interest anyone in following Jesus!"

I believe we've come a long way since then. I would rather attend a service of worship that is heavily populated by young people, than one which is heavily populated by my fellow "fat and forty-ish" friends. Youth ministries are just more interesting!

But "hype" is like sugar in your diet. A splash of it every now and again livens things up amazingly. Life gets a little dull without it. But if your **total** diet is sugar, then it won't build "fruit that will last". Feeding kids on sugar will always have 3 results

    i   an initial rush of energy
    ii then they will be flat
    iii then they will be fat.

That will never build "fruit that will last", will it?

I have been to youth ministries which seem to be **totally** run on hype.

> *"Let's have some crazy stunt games and we'll get the kids really hyped"*
>
> *"We'll have some outrageous praise music which will get the crowd really pumped"*

And of course, preachers can set out to deliberately "hype" a crowd to get a response. The right lighting, the right smoke machine; the PA set to a high level; the right music to set the "perfect mood", a few emotional stories. Its not hard to do. Just look at Hitler.

At Crossfire, we don't try to "hype" our students. We do try to make things as interesting as possible. We do lead enthusiastically. We aim to run things with excellence. But if our students want to be "mellow", that's fine with us. I know that if they only respond because they're "hyped up", their response will not last. That initial response which sugar brings may be exciting, but it will not be genuine. And if it's not genuine, it's not worth doing.

Sugar makes a diet interesting. Sprinkle it around sparingly to spice things up a little. But if your whole diet centres around it, you will not produce healthy fruit.

Hype can be a cheap substitute for "fruit that will last"

Cheap Substitute No. 4 - "Bait 'n' Switch"

Are you familiar with the old "bait 'n' switch" routine? It's where a certain product is advertised, and when the customer comes in to purchase it, an inferior product is substituted for it. Used only by the shonkiest of salesmen, it is totally unethical, and totally illegal.

Sometimes in our enthusiasm to get young people to come to our events, we can actually be guilty of a similar fraud. I have seen youth ministries which have "conned" students by not being up front about what they are inviting that student to.

> *"A drug and alcohol-free concert"*

That's what the poster said. It was describing a large Christian youth rally. Well, I guess in part it **was** a "drug and alcohol-free concert" but it was **also** a 40 minute sermon and a public invitation for students to give their life to Christ. Nothing wrong with that - hey, but let's not con students into thinking their only going to a "concert"

> *"Come along to our youth group! Fun, food, fantastic activities; it'll be a blast!"*

I would want that to be true of **all** Christian youth groups! But if you also have a half hour bible study, then shouldn't you mention it? When you invite students to your youth activities, do you give them a clear picture of what they're coming to? Or don't you trust the gospel that much? Are you still pulling "bait 'n' switch"? If your youth ministry came under the jurisdiction of the Department of Consumer Affairs, could you be prosecuted for false advertising?

When we challenge our Christian students to invite their unsaved friends to Crossfire, we tell them **not** to say *"Come to Crossfire! It's the greatest youth group in the world!"* (it probably isn't!). We challenge them to say *"Come to Crossfire! You'll discover the difference that Jesus can make to your life"*

That's why we run Crossfire. And we are not ashamed of Jesus. Or his gospel. Hopefully we can say along with the apostle Paul ...

> *"Therefore, since through God's mercy we have this ministry, we do not lose heart. Rather, we have renounced secret and shameful ways; we do not use deception, nor do we distort the word of God. On the contrary, by setting forth the truth plainly we commend ourselves to every man's conscience in the sight of God"* - **2 Corinthians 4: 1-2**

How do you think a student feels if he's come along to your youth event and he thinks it's "only a concert" - and discovers that it's also a full-blown sermon with altar call? How would you feel if you were "conned" in this way? I can guarantee that you wouldn't go back to that place in a hurry!

Don't use "bait 'n' switch". Jesus wouldn't.
Don't use "bait 'n' switch". It's unethical.

Don't use "bait 'n' switch". It's illegal.

Don't use "bait 'n' switch". It will never produce "fruit that will last".
It is a cheap and shonky substitute for quality fruit.

Cheap Substitute No. 5 -Picking Unripe Fruit

a) Be careful when you're aiming to reach crowds

Picture this. It's your big evangelistic night. Lots of students have come from all over. You have passionately proclaimed the message of Jesus. You have invited students to come forward and respond. You desperately want to see students come to Christ. You all sing a great "response song" and you wait for the crowds to push forward.

There's a small shuffle of feet. One or two students wander forward. But you are sure there are more. So you ask again. You sing another verse of the song. You implore. You plead. You get your keyboard player to just "tinkle" a little bit more on the piano. You really want to see kids - masses of kids - saved. You broaden your appeal. "If you just want to ask a question about Jesus - come out the front". "If you want to know how to spell the name 'Jesus' - come out the front".

Of course none of us would ever do that, would we? None of us would ever preach a "softer" message in the hope that more students will respond, would we? None of us would ever get our piano-player to play some "gooey" music so that students would feel more like responding, would we? None of us would ever tell an incredibly sad emotional story near the end so that students who were in tears would be more likely to come out the front, would we? None of us would ever broaden our appeal so much so that virtually everyone in the audience feels they've got to come out for one reason or another, would we? If we're serious about producing "fruit that will last" - here is one sure-fire way to blow it. Pick unripe fruit. If you pick unripe fruit, it will never have the quality and staying power that it is meant to have. If students only respond because we have pushed too hard, or cajoled too often, then their response will not be genuine. It will not last. It will not be genuine fruit. I would rather

FRUIT THAT WILL LAST

have **half** as many respond, and know that they were genuine, than to have a huge multitude respond simply because we had manufactured the environment to produce that response. Harvesting squillions of bits of fruit in one night might look impressive; but if it "goes off" after a couple of days, it wasn't worth it.

I can remember a weekend camp we had some years ago. It was our big "outreach event" for the year. Many of our Christian students invited their unsaved friends away for the weekend and were praying for them to respond. We got to the Sunday Morning meeting - where I publicly invited students to come forward and be saved. We started our final song.

"Come out and give your life to Jesus" I implored

We started singing. Nobody moved. Between the verses, I gave another quick invitation.

"if you want to say 'yes' to Jesus with your life, just come out the front"

We kept singing . Nobody moved.

While I led the singing from out the front, I had this incredibly quick and incredibly quiet conversation with God.

"Lord, this is a disaster! No-one's responding!"
"Why is it a disaster, Tim?"
"Cos I really want kids to be saved. And there's no-one coming out. This will look really bad"
"So, do you want kids to be saved, or do you want to look good?"
"Lord, you know what I really want is to see kids saved"
"Even if you look "bad"?"
"What do you mean, Lord"
"Is it okay with you if no-one comes forward today, but that in one week a whole stack of kids become Christians - by themselves - completely separate from you and your programme?"

I had to think for a moment. This was pushing all my buttons.

Eventually I knew deep down what I really wanted.

"Lord it is fine with me if no-one responds today, and you call students to follow you in a quieter less spectacular way"
"That's good Tim. I needed to know that. Now just invite them one more time"

I did. I issued one last invitation to respond. I held my breath. What would happen?

I couldn't believe the result. A whole row stood up and walked out the front. About 50 kids responded that day. Many many were saved, and lots of those are now working with me in youth ministry as leaders.

God had a few things he wanted to sort out with me that day. He wanted to know that I was in it for him and not just for me. He wanted to know that I was happy to do my part of the bargain (proclaim the message) and leave him to do his part (cause people to respond). A lot of people had their lives changed that day. I was one of them.

Don't pick unripe fruit! If you want to see "fruit that will last", then don't go brow-beating poor defenceless students into making a decision that they're not ready to make. I'm sure over the past 21 years I have talked more people out of becoming a Christian, than I have ever talked into it.

Do you want fruit that will last? Don't pick unripe fruit! What do you really want to be able to tell others?

"We had over 500 students respond to my message (but one year later most of them have fallen away)" ... or ...
"We had 50 students respond, and one year later they are all growing passionately as disciples"

Give me the latter any day!

b) Be careful when you're working with "just one"

Ivan* was a tough Year 9 boy at a tough Boy's High School. He used to sit in my Scripture Class, and often was the source of trouble. He was captain of the school football team, and his goal in life was to play representative rugby league for the district. He appeared to have very little interest in Christian things.

One week, on a Scripture worksheet that gave him the opportunity to give a personal response, he wrote down that he wanted to become a Christian. Quite frankly I don't think he understood what that meant. I caught up with him at lunchtime. I really didn't want him "making a decision" until he was truly ready. I didn't want to pick unripe fruit.

"So what's this about you wanting to become a Christian?" I enquired.
"That's right. I want to follow Jesus"

I thought he has having me on. I thought he was trying to make fun of me. I didn't think he really understood. So I decided to stop him in his tracks.

"You realise that if you become a Christian, that would mean that you would have to come to church"

Got him! There's no way out of this one. As soon as he sees that there's a real commitment involved here, he'll back right off.

"Yeah ... okay .. but what church should I go to?"

I hesitated.

"I guess you could come to church with me" I suggested
"What time is it?"
"7 o'clock Sunday Night"
"How would I get there?"
"I guess I could pick you up"
"Okay. here's my address. Is it okay if I bring a friend?"

I was flabbergasted. I went to pick him up that Sunday night. I never thought he would show. But he was there. Ready to go. With his friend. His mum asked me "What on earth did you say to my son to make him want to go to church? He's never been in his life!"

I smiled nervously. We all went to church. I chatted with him as I dropped him home

"You're really serious about this, aren't you?"
"Yeah. I want to come next week"
"How about we talk during the week, and catch up about things?"

I picked him up from school one afternoon that week, so we could talk. As we chatted, I still kept getting the impression that he did not understand what he was doing. I did not think he had any concept of treating Jesus as his Lord, or of submitting to him.

I was searching for what to say. I did not want to pick fruit that was unripe. He told me he had a girlfriend. So I pushed him on this.

"What if I told you that to start following Jesus you had to give up your girlfriend and never see her again?"

I wanted to challenge him on whether he was prepared to put Jesus No. 1. His answer was unexpected.

"O sure - no worries - I'll give her the flick straight away"

Hmmm. Australian men. They still don't know how to treat a lady. Wrong question. And then I hit on it! The perfect question.

"What if I were to tell you that to become a Christian, you had to give up playing rugby league, and never play it again?"

"Hmm ... that's a hard one"

We talked for the next half hour or so. We talked about the cost of being a committed follower of Jesus - we talked about the implications of having your whole life changed around by Christ.

Eventually, Ivan said

"If I've got to give up rugby league to follow Jesus I'm prepared to do it"

I knew he was ready. I led him to Christ, and sent him off to be the best rugby league player he could possibly be.

If you want to build "fruit that will last", then take the time to make sure you're not picking unripe fruit. Picking unripe fruit can be a cheap substitute for the real thing.

c) Be Careful with God's Gospel

Many years ago I went to a large evangelistic youth rally. Huge numbers. A top flight speaker. Here was his message. (grossly summarised by me!)

"Nothing in this world makes sense. Only Jesus does. No-one else has any answers. Jesus does. No-one else can fix your problems. Jesus can. Come forward and give your life to Jesus."

And hundreds did! Streams of young people went forward to give their life to Christ. And I have no doubt that many did - genuinely. I have no doubt that Christ was honoured in the lives of many of those young people.

But what on earth were they responding to? The gospel had not been mentioned! Without going into massive detail about "the gospel", it surely is the message about Jesus dying for our sins and being raised to give us life. There was nothing in his message about the death of Jesus; there was nothing about forgiveness of sins; indeed - there was nothing about our sin at all; there was nothing about Jesus' victory over the grave; there was nothing about the new life that Jesus has bought for us with the price of his own blood.

The message had been accidentally watered down to produce a greater response. But the response you get from this will never be one that lasts. If you are not careful to proclaim God's gospel, you will pick unripe fruit. You will never build "fruit that will last".

We know that the gospel is "the power of God so save all who believe" (Romans 1: 16-17). Think about this: If the gospel has not been proclaimed, and people respond, can you say that they've responded to the gospel? Look over this question again, and ask it slowly of yourself. "If the gospel has not been proclaimed, and people respond, can you say that they've responded to the gospel?"

Be careful with God's Gospel. Be careful with individuals . Be careful with a crowd. Don't run the risk of picking unripe fruit. It is a cheap substitute for "fruit that will last"

SECTION 2

How to Grow A Heart That Will Last

Chapter 4
Grow a Fully Devoted Heart

The next three chapters - indeed the whole of this section - "How to Grow a Heart That Will Last" contains the most vital section of this book. What I have learned about the state of my own heart has had more impact on the youth ministry that I have than any other factor. If my heart is not right ... my ministry will never be right. God still has much to teach me in this area.

Let's learn together.

1. Your Heart Really Matters To God

When the bible talks about your "heart" - it doesn't mean that small pump which keeps your blood supply racing around your body. The term "heart" means the absolute centre of your existence - where all your thoughts and desires start.

"Let's get to the heart of the problem" shows us how to use that word "heart"

*"Let's get to the **centre** of the problem"* is what we mean

"Let's get to the absolute core issue"

That's what God means too, when he talks about "your heart". The centre of your decision making. The absolute core of who you are. And who you really are really matters to God.

> *"The Lord does not look at the things man looks at. Man looks at the outward appearance, but the Lord looks at the heart"*
> ***1 Samuel 16:7***

You might think that how you're going as a youth leader will be judged by how good your programmes are, how many kids come along, how effective your preaching is. Wrong!

> *"The Lord does not look at the things man looks at. Man looks at the outward appearance, but the Lord looks at the heart"*
> **1 Samuel 16:7**

How you're going - deep inside - where maybe no-one else can see - that really matters to God.

2. Your Heart Is Not To Be Trusted

a) Given half a chance, it will do what is wrong.

How dangerous does God think the condition of your heart is?

> *"The Lord saw how great man's wickedness on the earth had become, and that every inclination of the thoughts of his heart was only evil all the time?"*
> **Genesis 6:5**

How dangerous does God think the condition of your heart is?

> *"The heart is deceitful above all things and beyond cure. Who can understand it?"*
> **Jeremiah 17:9**

I certainly can't understand my own heart! Sometimes I do things which are right out of character for someone who's passionately in love with Jesus. Sometimes I say things that are right out of character for someone's who's passionately in love with Jesus. Sometimes I think things which are right out of character for someone who's passionately in love with Jesus.

No wonder God urges me to guard my heart. Given half a chance, it will do what is wrong!

The heart of the human problem is the problem of the human heart.

b) It's where every sin starts

Every sin starts as a temptation. Every wrong action starts as a wrong thought. Every bit of evil in my life starts in my heart.

Here's an obvious example:

> *"But I tell you that anyone who looks at a woman lustfully has already committed adultery with her in his heart"*
> **Matthew 5:28**

Every wrong action starts as a wrong thought.

> *"But the things that come out of the mouth come from the heart, and these make a man 'unclean'. For out of the heart come evil thoughts, murder, adultery, sexual immorality, theft, false testimony, slander"*
> **Matthew 15:18**

Ouch! It makes you wonder why God doesn't give up on us! But he's promised to never do that. There is however another extreme problem with an unrepentant heart.

c) It could turn you away from God

What do you mean? Turn me away from God? I'm keen! I'm on fire! Once saved, always saved! I mean, I'm a youth pastor after all!

Maybe. But have you ever known of a Youth Pastor or Christian Youth Leader who walked away from Jesus? The history of Christian Youth Ministry is littered with the remains of unfaithful Christian Leaders who all said "It could never happen to me!"

God takes this danger seriously.

> *"See to it, brothers, that none of you has a sinful , unbelieving heart that turns away from the living God"*
> **Hebrews 3:12**

Remember, that verse was addressed to Christians! And if you still think you're somehow immune from turning your back on God, here is one more warning from God's Word:

> *"So, if you think you are standing firm, be careful that you don't fall"*
> **1 Corinthians 10:12**

d) Fix it up now before you go any further

Do you see how the state of your heart is so absolutely vital? It might be that there are things going on in your heart that you know are tearing you away from being a faithful follower of Jesus. There might be things that no-one else knows about.

Maybe now is the time to stop reading any further, and simply fall before your Lord in confession and repentance. God loves to see true confession. God loves to see true repentance.

> *"A broken and contrite heart, O God, you will not despise"*
> **Psalm 51:17**

If you have things to fix up with God, do it now before you proceed any further. Put down this book and pick up another one. Go to Psalm 51 in your bible. Sort things out with your creator. Go on! Don't worry! This book will still be here when you come back!

3. God Wants Your Heart Fully Devoted to Him

Two of the great leaders in the Old testament were King David, and his son, King Solomon. Here's a quick quiz for you. **What was the essential difference between them?** The kingdom prospered more under Solomon than it did under David. The kingdom was bigger, richer, attracted more crowds, had better buildings (the temple!) and became very much the centre of the known universe during Solomon's reign. So why is David remembered as the far better king?

What was the essential difference between the two of them?

It had to do with their hearts.

a) David was a man after God's own heart

Here is how David is described by God

> "I have found David, son of Jesse, **a man after my own heart** he
> will do everything I want him to do"
> **Acts 13:22**

God wants you to have a heart that is just like his. As big as his. As loving
as his. As pure as his.

b) When David sinned, he asked God to deal with his heart

But I can't be perfect!

No - having a heart like God's is not about being perfect. But it does have
to do with continuously turning back to him. And when you turn back to
him, then like David, ask him to deal with your heart

> "Create in me a pure heart, O God, and renew a steadfast spirit
> within me"
> **Psalm 51: 10**

c) David's desire was an undivided heart

A heart that is divided is a heart that is being pulled in two directions. It
is a heart that is being destroyed. Just ask a young man (or a young
woman) who has fallen in love with two different people at the same time!
A divided heart will never get you anywhere!

Listen carefully to what David really wants as he prays to his God.

> "Teach me your way, O Lord, and I will walk in your truth; give me an
> undivided heart, that I may fear your name"
> **Psalm 86:11**

What David really wanted was a heart that was totally devoted to serving
God. A heart that was not divided in any way. A heart that was one of
integrity - not of dis-integrity (or disintegration). That's why David's
leadership can be described in the following terms:

> *"David shepherded them with integrity of heart; with skilful hands he led them"*
> **Psalm 78:72**

d) The fatal problem of being "not fully devoted"

Solomon was a mighty king. A great ruler. Many fantastic things were achieved under his influence. He's the sort of bloke that most of us would have chosen as a Youth Pastor! But there is one statement in the bible that gets to the heart of his problem - and shows us the essential difference between David and Solomon.

> *"As Solomon grew old, his wives turned his heart after other gods, **and his heart was not fully devoted** to the Lord his God, as the heart of this father David had been"*
> **1 Kings 11:4**

His heart was not fully devoted to God. It was sort of devoted, but not fully devoted. It was a divided heart. It was a heart of dis-integrity.

4. Your heart will guide your ministry

If you do not have a heart of integrity, you will never have a ministry of integrity. The ministry that you have - the words that you speak - in the end can only come from a heart that is right with God.

> *"Out of the overflow of the heart, the mouth speaks"*
> **Matthew 12:34**

If you're faking it ... if you're pretending ... if you have a divided heart .. then you won't be able to fool people for long. You might look good for a while. But you will never build "fruit that will last"

5. So Guard Your Heart

Oh - if there's one thing us youth pastors and leaders need to work on - to work hard at - to work relentlessly at - is to guard our hearts. Because the work that God is doing **in** us is more important than the work he is doing **though** us. If you want to have a great ministry, before you put all your effort into building a bigger programme, or building bigger facilities, or building a better music ministry, or building a better P.R. department ... above all else, work hard to build a bigger heart.

> *"Above all else, guard your heart, for it is the wellspring of life"*
> **Proverbs 4:23**

Because as you let God build a bigger heart in you, you will discover that he is also able to build a bigger ministry to flow through you.

Ask God to search your heart, and to change anything which is a barrier to your being the person that he wants you to be.

> *"Search me, O God, and know my heart; test me and know my anxious thoughts. See if there is any offensive way in me, and lead me in the way everlasting"*
> **Psalm 139: 23-24**

Chapter 5

Grow a Disciple's Heart

If you want to be used in a "big-time" way by God, then you need to let him work "big-time" in your own life. He wants to see you as a faithful disciple first; then you will be ready to be used by him as a pastor or leader.

It took a long time for me to learn this. When I first started as a full-time youth pastor in 1978, I was full of the excitement of the job. There was a church to familiarise myself with; there were students to get to know; there was a programme to run. Full of excitement, I threw myself headlong into that ministry. Lots of great things were happening, but it was kinda shallow, and I was left feeling kinda dry. I had let my enthusiasm for youth ministry run ahead of my own personal enthusiasm to be a disciple of Jesus. It was not until I was humbled before God's word that God started to work through me in a deep and impactful way!

If you want impact, you gotta go for intimacy. The single most determining factor in how impactful I have been in ministry for Jesus, has to do with how intimate I have been with Jesus himself.

Together, let's develop the heart of a disciple.

1. 3 steps to growing a disciple's heart

a) Keep growing deeper into the vine.

There is a magnificent picture in John 15 of the joy and intimacy of being a disciple. It is the picture of a vine growing strongly, with numerous branches spurting out - also growing strongly. If you're not familiar with what a grapevine looks like, then try and imagine a tree trunk, with many branches sprouting out. It's the same picture.

Have a read through John 15: 1-8. (read further if you're game). Can you see the intimacy of the relationship between the branches and the vine?

Time and time again, Jesus says to us "remain in me" (John 15: 4, 5, 6, 7) That word "remain" doesn't sound very powerful. But it's meant to be. Even the old word "dwell" doesn't capture the picture well because that word is not used much more. But try and picture this. Jesus is talking about "making our home" in him. "Sinking our foundations" into him. "Plugging in" to him like you plug a TV into a power point.

Because when you're "plugged in" to Jesus in that way, can you see that the very lifestream that flows through Jesus will also flow through you? You will start to reproduce in your life the very character of Jesus himself! Wow!

> "No branch can bear fruit by itself; it must remain in the vine"
> **John 15:4**

> "If a man remains in me, and I in him, he will bear much fruit; apart from me you can do nothing"
> **John 15:5**

Imagine the foolishness of a branch lying on the ground by itself saying "If I work really hard on this, I can grow! Come on fruit - out you come". It is a silly picture. A branch lying on the ground by itself cannot achieve anything. It will wither and die. Its only use is to be burned for firewood. To be alive - to be fruitful - that branch must be intimately connected to the vine.

But I know of "Christians" who attempt to grow "by themselves". Sadder than that, I know of youth pastors who try to carry out an impactful ministry without safeguarding their own intimacy with Jesus.

Hang out with Jesus. Worship Jesus. Love Jesus. Read Jesus' word. Pray to Jesus. Sink your foundations deeper into Jesus. Get immersed in Jesus. Be surrounded by him and engulfed by him.

If you want to grow passionate disciples amongst your youth, you need to be a growing, passionate disciple yourself. You will always reproduce after your own kind. You cannot take your students where you yourself are not prepared to go.

b) Keep growing deeper into the whole tree

I guess nearly every time I look at John 15, I interpret it in an individual way. Jesus is the vine, and I am the one solitary branch that needs to remain plugged into him.

If that was what this vine was really like, can I suggest it would be a pretty sick vine? Imagine a tree with only one branch! It's a ridiculous picture. But no more ridiculous than my interpretation of John 15 that only sees the passage in an individual way.

Sure. John 15 is a call for individual intimacy between the individual believer and Jesus. But the picture is of a complete vine - a complete tree. One with lots and lots and lots of branches!

Jesus does not say "I am the vine - you are the **branch**"

He says "I am the vine. You are the **branches**"

In the good old King James Version, it reads this way:

"I am the vine; **ye** are the branches"

We don't have a good, modern English word to describe the plural of "you"

But the word here for "you" **is** plural.

Aussie slang might put it this way

"I am the vine. **Youse** are the branches.

Or .. "I am the vine; **You lot** are the branches"

If you want to develop the heart of a disciple. then you've gotta make sure you are absolutely plugged into the body of believers. Just as you need to draw on the very lifestream that flows through Christ, then you also need to draw from the very lifestream that flows through the other believers as well.

What would you say to a student who said "I'm a Christian now. I don't need to come to church or a bible study group". You would be horrified! "Of course you need to come to church and bible study! How else will you grow and learn from all the other believers?"

What would you say to a youth pastor or youth leader who doesn't see the need to learn from other believers and fellowship with them? Cos I've seen it happen. Good youth pastors who are still flying solo, wondering why they are starting to feel a little bit drained.

Is there a bible study group you can belong to (one where **you** don't have to lead all the time)? Is there a prayer triplet you can link up with? Are there some fellow youth pastors that you can be involved with for mutual growth and support? Is there a wise and godly man or woman who can be a mentor for you?

God has provided you with this most marvellous resource - the family of God's people who are there to refresh you and enliven you.

If you want to develop the heart for basketball, hang out with basketballers.

If you want to develop the heart for gardening, hang out with gardeners.

If you want to develop the heart of a disciple, hang out with other disciples.

Go on! You might just enjoy it!

c) Be prepared to be pruned

It's a lot of fun hanging out with Jesus. It's a lot of fun hanging out with other believers. But if you really want to be fruitful - there's a third step mentioned here, which on the outside doesn't always look like it's going to be that enjoyable.

> *"while every branch that does bear fruit he prunes so that it will be even more fruitful"*
> ***John 15:2***

Ouch! Imagine God pruning you! But that's what he'll do **not to punish you but to make you more fruitful!**

I don't know much about gardening, but I know this much. If you want your plant to produce more fruit (or more flowers), you cut off the sections of the plant that are not productive. You prune back the rough edges so that all the energy of that plant can be directed towards producing fruit (or flowers as the case may be)

The same is true with God. He wants you to be fruitful. He wants you to be fruitful in your personal life. He wants you to be fruitful in your ministry. He wants to prune you so you will be more and more fruitful. He wants to cut off every area of your life that is unproductive. He wants to chop off things that you are doing that are stopping you from being the person he has destined you to be. And he wants to do this because he loves you and wants you to achieve the absolute maximum for you that is possible.

Are you ready for God to prune you? Are you prepared to surrender to him anything about your life that is not bearing fruit - and for God to get rid of it? Do you honestly want God to take away anything that you're into which is stopping from being more and more Christlike? That's what God wants to do in your life. Is that what **you** want him to do?

Pruning can be painful. What needs to go? An independent attitude? A secret sin? An inappropriate relationship? An unhelpful pastime? A bitter tongue? An unforgiving heart? What is it?

If you want to develop the heart of a disciple, then let God, as the skilful surgeon, cut away anything that will give you heart disease.

2. 3 results of growing a disciple's heart

a) You will bear much fruit

There are huge rewards when you grow the heart of a disciple. This passage from John 15 is full of the excitement of reaping the benefits that flow from being in step with Jesus.

The whole passage is about being fruitful. The whole point of developing the heart of a disciple is that you will bear more fruit.

> *"every branch that does bear fruit he prunes so that it will be even more fruitful"*
> ***John 15:2***

"neither can you bear fruit unless you remain in me"
John 15:4

So, what is this "fruit" that God is so keen for you to bear?

i The evidence of the life of Jesus in you

I'm not much of a gardener at all. Nearly everything I touch in the garden dies. My basic philosophy of gardening is "Survival of the Fittest". If it thrives, it deserves to thrive; if it dies, it deserves to die; if it gets out of control, I mow it. I will never win a gardening prize. They will never name a TV show after me and call it "Tim's Backyard".

But the first Youth Pastor's position I ever had was in a delightful part of the world called South Australia. South Australia is a huge fruit-growing area, and the house I moved into had a veritable orchard in the backyard. There were fruit trees everywhere! I didn't even know what most of them were!

But there was one tree in the middle of the backyard that took pride of place. And even with my stunted gardening knowledge, I was immediately able to deduce that this was an orange tree!

Now ... how was I - a mere novice - able to determine that this particular tree was indeed an orange tree? **Because it had oranges growing on it!** The oranges were the visible evidence that this was indeed an orange tree. The orange fruit proved to me that "orange life" was running through that tree. And because "orange life" was running though that tree, then I knew I wouldn't find watermelons, or bananas, or pineapples growing from that same tree. It was an orange tree! The orange fruit that was growing on it was a sure sign of the orange life that flowed through it.

The same is true of you. When you have the very lifestream of Jesus flowing through you, it will show itself in all sort of ways throughout your life. In fact anything that is visible evidence of the "Jesus life" that flows through you could be described as being the "fruit" of a disciple. If you are indeed growing the heart of a disciple ... if you are committed to having the very lifestream of Jesus flowing through you ... if you are open to God pruning you to make you more and more fruitful, then this "fruit" will show itself in the following ways:

ii   The evidence of the character of Jesus in you

The main "fruit" or "evidence" that Jesus wants to see in your life is a changed character. Galatians 5 gives us the clues as to what this will look like. A disciple who is bearing the fruit of a changed character will have a life that is dominated by ... "love, joy, peace, patience, kindness, goodness, faithfulness, gentleness and self control" (Galatians 5: 22-23)

Why is this the "fruit" of a spirit-filled, Christ-controlled person? Because that is the character of Jesus himself. When you get to know Jesus in a deep and personal way, you will discover what his character is like. You will discover that Jesus keeps showing ... "love, joy, peace, patience, kindness, goodness, faithfulness, gentleness and self control"

When people look at you, do they see the character of Christ?

Because if we're not careful, we can end up looking like "fruit-salad" Christians. We can show all sorts of different fruit - much of it contradictory, much of it confusing.

Imagine how surprised I would have been to see that my orange tree start to grow other fruit ... tomatoes ... lychees ... pears etc. I would have thought that I was going crazy! I would have had real doubts as to whether it was a genuine orange tree or not!

Wouldn't it be confusing if other people saw contradictory "fruit" in your life. Galatians 5 tells us about another sort of "fruit". "sexual immorality, impurity and debauchery; idolatry and witchcraft; hatred, discord, jealousy, fits of rage, selfish ambition, dissensions, factions and envy; drunkenness, orgies, and the like" (Galatians 5: 19-21)

When people look at you, do they see the fruit - the character - of Christ?

Even when no-one is watching, do you display the fruit - the character - of Jesus?

What sort of a person do you want to be known as? It is your fruit that will establish your character with the world. It is your character that will establish your ministry with the world. It is by your fruit that you will be known

"By their fruit you will recognise them. Do people pick grapes from thornbushes, or figs from thistles? Likewise every good tree bears good fruit, but a bad tree bears bad fruit. A good tree cannot bear bad fruit, and a bad tree cannot bear good fruit. Every tree that does not bear good fruit is cut down and thrown into the fire. Thus, by their fruit you will recognise them."
Matthew 7: 16-22

The first step to producing fruit that will last in your ministry is producing fruit that will last in your life. Because it's what's in your heart that will be reproduced in the hearts of your kids.

iii The evidence of the ministry of Jesus in you

If the first part of "fruit" is your Christlike character, then the second part is your Christlike ministry.

"You did not choose me, but I chose you and appointed you to go and bear fruit - fruit that will last"
John 15:16

There is a reason for Jesus choosing you. He has appointed you to "go and bear fruit - fruit that will last". When Jesus says "go" - he's normally talking about "going and having a ministry". God is very much into "going". Two thirds of God's name is "Go"!

The evidence for the ministry that you have will be the lives of the students you minister to. I can often tell how any of our "D-team Coaches" are going (home bible study leaders – see details in Chapters 14 and 15). I simply look at the "fruit" of their ministry. That is, I look at the lives of the students that they are training as disciples. I know some leaders will have "difficult" students to work with. I don't expect to see "results" all the time. But the lives of their students will be one of the indicators that tells me how they are going in ministry.

The key challenge that Jesus gives here about the "fruit" of your ministry - will it be "fruit that will last"? How will your students stand for Christ after they have left the protective environment of your youth ministry?

"Fruit that will last" - sounds like a good title for a book! The rest of this book will show you how to have an effective youth ministry so that you do indeed produce "fruit that will last"

But before we move on to that, don't forget this main result of growing a disciple's heart - that you will bear fruit. Fruit in your personal life; fruit in your ministry.

But wait - there's more!

Here are 2 more results of growing a disciple's heart.

b) Your prayers will be answered

It couldn't be clearer.

> *"If you remain in me, and my words remain in you, ask whatever you wish, and it will be given you"*
> ### John 15:7

A second result of growing a disciple's heart - of sinking deeper into Jesus and feeding from his very lifestream - is "ask whatever you wish, and it will be given you" .When you grow a disciple's heart, there is the promise that your prayers will be answered.

How so?

Think about it. What sort of things will a branch ask a vine for? It will only ask for those things that will make the branch fruitful, to benefit the whole tree.

You will notice a change in your prayers as you grow a disciple's heart. You will change the way your pray. You will pray more and more for things that will make you more fruitful, and you will pray for things that will bless and encourage the whole body. You will stop praying for things that have nothing to do with your fruitfulness; you will stop praying for things that have nothing to do with growing the body.

You will find that you are starting to pray for the things that Jesus would pray for. That's what it means by praying "in Jesus' name". And because you are praying for those things that you know Jesus would ask for, you will find that your prayers are indeed being answered.

When I was a boy, every now and again our family would have to make an emergency purchase. Sometimes I would arrive home from school with my school shoes absolutely falling to pieces. I simply had to have a new pair of shoes straight away. Mum would send me down to the store - with her store credit card - and a signed note saying something like "Please supply my son with a pair of black leather school shoes - no more than $20 - and charge it to my account".

The people at the store knew my mum. They would give me the shoes and charge it to her account. They knew that everything was "above board". School shoes are the sort of things that my mum would ask for.

Imagine what would have happened if I showed up to the store - with my mum's credit card - and a note that said something like "Please supply my son with all the chocolate he wants - and charge it to my account"! I imagine that the salesperson would be immediately suspicious, and would phone my mum to check if this were a genuine request. I would not get the chocolate I wanted because the salesperson would know that I was asking for something that was **not** the sort of thing my mother would ask for or authorise.

Check out your prayers. Are you asking for the sorts of things that Jesus would ask for? Because as you sink deeper and deeper into Jesus - as you develop the heart of a disciple - then the more you will ask for things in your prayers that God loves to say "yes" to.

What are you praying for yourself? What are you praying for your ministry? Develop the heart of a disciple - it will change your prayers - and you will see rich answers from our heavenly God who loves to say "yes".

c) God will be glorified

> *"This is to my father's glory, that you bear much fruit, showing yourselves to be my disciples"*
> ***John 15:8***

This is the greatest result of being a "fruitful disciple' - **God is glorified!** That's right! When you develop the heart of a disciple - when you sink deeply into Jesus - and when your bear more and more fruit, your father God is glorified.

How?

> *"I am the true vine, and my father is the gardener. He cuts off every branch in me that bears no fruit, while every branch that does bear fruit he prunes so that it will be even more fruitful."*
> ***John 15: 1-2***

When you become a fruitful branch, your father God gets the glory because he is the gardener!

It's the county fair. All the country folk have come in from miles around for a weekend of celebration. One of the central competitions is the pumpkin growing challenge. All the pumpkin growers of the district have lined up their prize exhibits. The judges have conferred, and first prize is awarded to Mrs MacGillicuddy's prize pumpkin.

Who gets the honour? Who gets the glory? Do the judges come up and say "O great pumpkin - here is your prize. You are a magnificent specimen. I have never met a pumpkin as robust as you. I want to give you all the honour and all the praise. Tell me, what's the secret of your success?"

No! It's not the pumpkin who gets the prize! It's not the pumpkin who gets the glory! It's Mrs MacGillicuddy who gets all the honour and all the attention because she is the gardener who has produced such a magnificent specimen. She is honoured for being the best gardener in the land.

When you bear fruit in your life - when you bear fruit in your ministry - when you bear "fruit that will last" - God is glorified because he is the gardener. He is the one who has produced this fruit because of his skilful pruning. He gets the prize. He gets the glory. He is honoured as being the best gardener in the land.

That's why you exist. So that God will be honoured as you bear fruit in your life. Do you want God to be glorified? Then keep growing deeper into Jesus. Allow yourself to be pruned. Produce great fruit in your personal life. Bear much fruit in your ministry. Develop the heart of a disciple. Bear "fruit that will last"

And God **will** be glorified!

Chapter 6
Grow a Pastor's Heart

One of the traps of youth ministry is you can just end up running a programme. Perhaps it's a good programme, but you get the feeling that week in, week out, you simply churn the old youth group through once again. You used to have the enthusiasm - but somehow it's not quite there any more.

How do you make sure that you're having a real ministry - building "fruit that will last", rather than just running a youth programme. I can assure you - a mere programme - no matter **how** good it is - no matter how many resources you throw at it - a programme does not have the ability to build "fruit that will last".

We know that the gospel has the power to save those who believe. But it is not a mechanical thing. Otherwise we could just make a recording of the gospel, and keep playing it over and over again, knowing that those whom God had chosen would respond. There isn't a technique that gets people to become Christians. There isn't a course that grows Christians and makes them strong. God uses **people** to communicate his message of undying love. God uses **pastors** to inspire and equip these people to have a personal ministry that will impact others.

Think about the time when you became a Christian.. or a time when you grew as a Christian .. or a time when you dealt with some personal issue which unleashed you for a stronger level of obedience. Can you think of a time like that? When you think of the times when God has significantly impacted and altered the direction of your growth - you will probably find that at the centre of that growth there was another **person** who really cared about you. There were **people** who took the time to get to know you, and listen to you, and encourage you, and correct you, and help you get back on the right path.

Someone who was a good friend. Someone who was a caring pastor.

True?

In the bible, the image of a pastor - or a shepherd - is a very powerful one. Think of every picture you can from the bible that involves a shepherd. They are bold pictures - a shepherd laying down his life for his sheep - a shepherd protecting his sheep from the wolves. They are also caring pictures - rescuing the lost sheep - guiding his sheep to green pastures and quiet waters - the loving shepherd binding up the wounds of his sheep and carrying it under his arm.

If you can visualise these pictures, then you can understand what it means to grow the heart of a shepherd - or the heart of a pastor. The word "pastor" simply means "shepherd", and the bible is full of pictures to guide you as you grow your heart.

How do you grow a pastor's heart? I want to have a look at one of the great pastors in the New Testament - the Apostle Paul.

Try and picture the apostle Paul. From anything you know about him - from any story you can remember - what sort of picture do you get of him? I get a hard-nosed, full-on, "take no prisoners" sort of bloke ... full of passion ... full of fire ... charging forward at any cost.

I picture him breathing murderous threats against the disciples as he charges off to Damascus (Acts 9) ... I can see him confronting the sorcerer - accusing him of being a child of the devil, and calling on God to strike him blind (Acts 13) ... I can visualise him being chased out of town after town as he boldly proclaimed the risen Christ .. I can see him in sharp disagreement with Barnabus (Acts 15); singing hymns at midnight and being miraculously freed from prison (Acts 16); and consistently being hauled before tribunals and courts as his proclamation of Jesus led to arguments and riots.

And every young hot-blooded youth pastor says "Yes Lord! I want to be like that!" But if we only see Paul's **passion** as a pastor, and miss his **heart** as a pastor, then we will launch ourselves on an unsuspecting world with all guns blazing and simply destroy every ministry that we put our hand to.

I've seen it happen too many times. Young pastors come to a church with "I've just finished bible college so I know everything" disease, and within 6 months, they have made such an impact at that church that everybody wants to get rid of them!

If you really want to have a ministry with impact, you must develop the heart of a pastor. How do you grow a pastor's heart? I want to have a look at one of the great pastors in the New Testament - the Apostle Paul. As he chats with the Christians in Thessalonica, he will reveal 5 key steps to growing a pastor's heart.

1. Care Gently

> "As apostles of Christ, we could have been a burden to you, but we were gentle among you, like a mother caring for her little children"
> *1 Thessalonians 2: 6-7*

What an amazing picture! The mighty apostle Paul describes his relationship with the Christians at Thessalonica as being "gentle ... like a mother caring for her little children". If you've had children, you will understand this picture. Imagine a little baby, nursing at his mother's breast. Picture the toddler, taking his first faltering footsteps. Imagine the hungry child, unable to feed himself, totally dependent on caring parents to survive and grow. Imagine a developing child, discovering the universe by asking his mum "why?" thousands upon thousands of times every day.

Are you starting the get an idea of a pastor's heart? We are the ones who give milk to baby Christians so they will start to grow; we guide the early steps of each new believer so they do not fall into danger; we care for students who are not yet ready to "go it alone" in this harsh world: we help young people to live a life of active ministry by showing them the "why" behind this universe that God has made.

What a thrill to be a youth pastor! But the challenge to building a pastor's heart is to **care** gently. Sensitively. By looking after people. Stopping and caring for them. Gentle like a mum with her little baby.

Does that describe the way you deal with people? Is it a picture of how you interact with your leaders? Does it accurately sum up how you care for those students who never seem to be able to co-operate with what your youth group is doing? When folk in your church are discussing you, do words like "gentle" and "caring" keep featuring?

Because that's what Jesus is like. Gentle. Caring. He is described this way: *"A bruised reed he will not break, and a smouldering wick he will not snuff out (Isaiah 42:3) "Your king comes to you, gentle, and riding on a donkey: (Matthew 21:5)* Jesus himself invites us *"Take my yoke upon you and learn from me, for I am gentle and humble in heart" (Matthew 11:29)*

Jesus stood up to the false teachers of his day. He challenged injustice wherever he saw it. He threw out those who were despising God and turning his temple into a rip-off palace. And yet he shows us the heart of a pastor. He shows us the gentle caring of a mum for her baby. He cries over his people who are rejecting him.

> *"O Jerusalem, Jerusalem, you who kill the prophets and stone those sent to you, how often I have longed to gather your children together, as a hen gathers her chicks under her wings, but you were not willing"*
> **Matthew 23:37**

Every youth pastor has seen the distress of young people who walk away from Jesus. You have wanted to gather them under your wings like a mother hen. But they would not come.

The first step to developing the heart of a pastor is to learn to care gently.

2. Love Genuinely

> *"We loved you so much that we were delighted to share with you not only the gospel of God but our own lives as well, because you had become so dear to us."*
> **I Thessalonians 2:8**

Do you catch the joyful love that Paul had developed for the people he had ministered to him? If you can learn to genuinely love those who are in your care, you will be unleashed into such a joy of ministry that it will be impossible to hold you back!

There are some days when I don't feel like going to work. I don't want to have to put the hard work in to prepare a sermon. I listen to people and I'm not particularly interested. I put up with students when I would rather be snuggled up at home with my favourite TV show. All youth pastors probably have days like that.

But imagine ministering **every day** like that! Imagine being a youth pastor or a youth leader and never developing the love of a pastor for his people. If you want to grow a pastor's heart, you must learn to love personally.

Look at the results!

a) You will enjoy your ministry

> *"We loved you so much that we were delighted to share with you ..."*

Do you delight in sharing ministry with the students in your youth group? When you learn to love someone genuinely, serving them becomes a delight.

> When I was a young boy, the whole "dating" thing seemed silly to me. Why would a young man spend his hard-earned money to take a girl out? Why did the guy have to pay? What a sad use of money! But now I am married ... now I have a fantastic wife whom I genuinely love ... I am **delighted** to spend money on her! Nothing could please me more than to be able to serve her!

When you learn to love those whom you serve, ministry becomes a delight and a joy.

b) You will want to share God's Gospel

> *"We loved you so much that we were delighted to share with you not only the gospel of God..."*

You know the power of the gospel. You know it can save all those who believe. The message of Jesus' death and resurrection has life-giving power, and has transformed the lives of millions around the planet.

You know this. You're convinced of this.

So how come I keep coming across youth ministries that are scared to share the gospel? They don't want to "turn students off" or "get them offside". So they water down the message and only go for trendy "youth" topics that never go anywhere near the gospel ("Peer Pressure - Part 26"). They give up preaching. They give up bible studies. They opt for a social programme and console themselves with the thought that "at least the young people are coming along".

If you genuinely love students, you will be **delighted** to share the gospel with them.

So how come you're sometimes reluctant to share this good news with others? Sure - when you've got your professional "Christian Youth Pastors' Badge" on, you will share the gospel. But what about when you're just seen as an average citizen? With your neighbours? With your old mates from school? With your friends on the soccer team?

There might be many complex answers to this, but let me tell you where it starts. If you learn genuine love for those around you - to see them as Christ would see them, then you **will not be able to hold back** from sharing the gospel with them. In a world of dying people - where you have the words of eternal life - the most loving thing you can do is to share that life-giving message with others.

But as powerful and important as the gospel is, genuine love will also unleash you to share something else that is extremely valuable and precious.

c) You will want to share your own life

> *"We loved you so much that we were delighted to share with you not only the gospel of God but our own lives as well .."*

When you develop a genuine love for your students, you will find that you want to share your life with them. You'll have them involved in your life - and you'll get involved with their life. If you're committed to loving the leaders that you work with, then you'll get them involved with your life -

and you'll get involved with their life.

i   "Warts and All" Love

This is scary stuff! When you share your life with someone - they see what you're really like - warts and all!

> I remember having some senior high students in my car with me. They were part of my discipleship group, and we had been learning and growing together for some years. I had been trying to model for them about how to be a Christlike disciple.
>
> The road was wet - and the car in front of me suddenly pulled up. I hit the brakes hard - and my car started aquaplaning and skidding straight towards the car in front. I had no control. A smash looked certain.
>
> I wrestled with the wheel - applied the brakes - trying to do **something** that would avert disaster. In that nanosecond that I had to react, a very loud word exploded from my mouth. It was a word that was probably not a great model of Christlikeness.
>
> I don't think the students could believe what they heard. This wasn't the "public image" of the youth pastor that everyone else saw. By getting them involved in my life, I was opening myself up to them warts and all. I managed to avoid a crash that day, but I couldn't avoid what had come out of my mouth. My students got to see the rougher side of my humanity, but more importantly, they learned how to deal with things when you get it wrong.

When you share your life with someone - they see what you're really like - warts and all!

ii Costly love

Sharing your life with someone can also be costly. Jesus certainly found it costly to share his life with us! His genuine love for us - his pastor's heart - took him to death on a cross.

"I am the good shepherd. The good shepherd lays down his life for the sheep"
John 10:11

When you open your life to the people that you minister to, it is a costly exercise. You never know where it might take you.

It was Monday about tea-time when the phone rang. It was **Glen's*** mum. She was down at the police station. Glen had been arrested for attempting to murder his father. He had stabbed his father 9 times, and his dad was now in a critical condition in hospital. Could I come down to the police station?

As I sped down in the car, a thousand thoughts raced through my head. How? Why? What? Glen was a Year 10 student, and a member of a discipleship group which I led. He had been coming along to the youth group for the last few years. He was one of the nicest, quietest, most co-operative kids that we had. Hardly a mean streak in him. How could he attack his dad?

The following weeks revealed a history of abuse that had pushed Glen to the limit. He had struck back for the first time in his life - and had gone way over the top. He was charged with attempted murder, and the court case was obviously going to be drawn out and involved.

He couldn't return home. Going away to relatives would have taken him away from his community and his support structures. Staying locked up would have destroyed him. So what did genuine love mean in my ministry as a youth pastor? It meant that Karen and I took Glen into our house and he lived with us for 3 years.

Genuine love is always costly. There was a real cost in having Glen move in with us. There was a cost on our lifestyle; there was a cost on our family; there was a cost on our marriage. True love always has a high price. If you want to develop a pastor's heart, you need to be prepared for the cost of developing genuine love.

iii A cheaper alternative

If all that sounds too costly, there is a cheaper alternative.

> "I am the good shepherd. The good shepherd lays down his life for the sheep. The hired man is not the shepherd who owns the sheep. So when he sees the wolf coming, he abandons the sheep and runs away. Then the wolf attacks the flock and scatters it. The man runs away because he is a hired hand and cares nothing for the sheep"
>
> **John 10: 11-13**

If it's too costly to show the genuine love of a true shepherd or pastor, there is another way that you can be a youth leader. You could just be a hired hand. There's a job to be done. So you do it. Maybe you get paid. Maybe you don't. But you are a youth leader at your church "because you got asked" "because all your friends are" "because someone's got to do it"

If your involvement with youth is "just a job" "just a ministry you'll do for a year or two" "just a fill-in" - then you are not a shepherd - you are a hired hand. You don't have a genuine love for your sheep - you're just doing your job. And if it gets too hard, you'll back off and go and do something else. If the kids get a bit ratty - then you'll leave them to their own devices. If someone's in real trouble, then like the pharisee or the priest, you can "pass by on the other side" whilst you pray the devout prayer of "Be warmed. Be filled".

No genuine love. No lasting commitment. But don't fool yourself. You are not a pastor. You are not a shepherd. You are a hired hand. You have not developed a pastor's heart. You have not learned genuine love.

And you will never produce "fruit that will last".

3. Work Hard

a) Work is a four letter word

> *"Surely you remember, brothers, our toil and hardship; we worked night and day in order not to be a burden to anyone while we preached the gospel of God to you"*
> ***1 Thessalonians 2:9***

Ouch! That sentence contains a few words guaranteed to trouble the heart of any fun-lovin' youth leader. Words like "toil" "hardship" "work". Ugghh!! You didn't get into youth ministry because you wanted "toil" or "hardship" or "work"!

But if you want to produce "fruit that will last" ... if you want to be a "good shepherd" ... there is no doubt that it will be hard work. There are no short cuts. If you want to have lasting impact through your youth ministry, you need to be prepared to put in the hard yards.

b) Big results need a big effort

The bible is full of pictures that show us the importance of hard work

> *"Endure hardship with us like a good soldier of Christ Jesus. No one serving as a soldier gets involved in civilian affairs - he wants to please his commanding officer. Similarly, if anyone competes as an athlete, he does not receive the victor's crown unless he competes according to the rules. The hard working farmer should be the first to receive a share of the crops."*
> ***2 Timothy 2: 3-6***

There are 3 pictures presented here. The soldier ... the athlete ... the farmer. There are all sorts of differences amongst these images, but here is one thing that is true of all of them - **they all involve hard work**. If you want to produce "fruit that will last".. if you want to receive a "share of the crops" - then you need to be prepared to be a "hard working farmer". The only place where "success" comes before "work" is in the dictionary!

c) Be faithful in the small things

You see, there's sort of a "sparkling attraction" about youth ministry. It looks cool. It looks like fun. There's a challenge to get a wayward teenager to go down the straight and narrow. The spotlight is focussed on the youth worker who can succeed where others have failed. It's easy to want to be the youth speaker who can captivate a crowd of 1000. It's great to think that you can run a successful camp for 200 teenagers. It's an appealing relationship to have a teenager pouring out their heart and soul to you when they have put the shutters up to everybody else.

But if you haven't learned to work hard as a servant, even the most glorious "up front" ministry will never produce fruit that will last. It might produce fast fruit - but not lasting fruit. And it could well be that God wants you to spend some time growing a servant's heart - and being faithful in "small things" - where there's no spotlight and no applause - so that he might prepare you for the "big things" he has in mind.

> *"Whoever can be trusted with very little can also be trusted with much ..."*
> **Luke 16:10**

Do you want to be trusted by God with "big things"? Then be faithful with the "small things" he has given in to your charge.

d) The Servant Squad

One of our leadership training strategies at Crossfire is what we call "The Servant Squad". We run a large week-long discipleship camp during the summer holidays. About 200 high-schoolers would attend. We have a leadership team of 50 or 60. You can imagine, with those sorts of numbers, there is a multitude of tasks that need to be done each day simply so a community of 250 can survive. Kitchens need to be cleaned after each meal; the auditorium needs to be set up each day; food needs to be carried; trenches need to be dug around tents; luggage needs to be transported ... the list is endless.

We take away with us some students who have just graduated from high school - and they become our "Servant Squad". These are the students whom we want to train as leaders. These are the ones we believe will have dynamic and impactful ministries for Christ in the future. We want to develop and train them to be the best youth leaders that they can be.

We start by teaching them servanthood. They do all those nuts-and-bolts things around camp that need to be done. The unspectacular jobs. The ones that no - one notices. The ones that no-one wants to do. We want to train them to have servant hearts - and be prepared to work hard. We want to train them to be faithful in the "small things" - so that God will be able to use them to achieve "big things".

Do you want to develop the heart of a pastor? Then be prepared to work hard. It is **always** worth it!

> *"Always give yourself fully to the work of the Lord, because you know that your labour in the Lord is not in vain"*
> ***1 Corinthians 15:58***

4. Live with Integrity

> *"You are witnesses, and so is God, of how holy, righteous and blameless we were among you who believed"*
> ***1 Thessalonians 2:10***

This is a huge topic - and absolutely crucial to developing the heart of a pastor. You cannot produce a ministry of integrity unless you are living a life of integrity. This is covered in depth in other parts of this book.

However, check this out:

a) **Your students are your witnesses**

When Paul wants accountability of his integrity, he asks the people he has been ministering to. "I've worked with you. I've ministered with you. Do you think I was 'holy, righteous and blameless'?"

Your students are always watching you. They see what you do. They hear what you say. They notice how you handle success. They observe how you deal with failure. They know what your "public image" is like -

and they see you when your guard is down.

Every step you take. Every move you make. Someone is watching. And learning. And imitating.

No wonder the bible says:

> "Not many of you should presume to be teachers (or youth leaders!), my brothers, because you know that we who teach will be judged more strictly'
> **James 3:1**

If we asked your students to testify to your integrity, would they use words like "holy, righteous and blameless"?

b) God is your witness

I'm not sure I would be as brave as Paul in calling God as a character witness. Paul is convinced that God himself will testify that he is in fact "holy, righteous and blameless". I know that God knows everything about me. He even knows the things that am hiding from myself. But knowing that God **is** my witness encourages me to keep my personal standards high even when no-one else is watching.

Who you are "when no-one is looking" really matters.

c) Your character

"Holy, righteous and blameless" describe your character. If you want to produce "fruit that will last', if you want to develop a pastor's heart, then you need to develop the Christlikeness of your character.

Have a look at the qualities of a leader that are in the 4 lists in the bible. (1 Timothy 3: 1-7, 1 Timothy 3: 8-13, 2 Timothy 2: 22-26, Titus 1: 5-9). Work out how many of these things are "gifts or abilities", and how many of them have to do with personal character. **Over 90% of things in these lists have to do with Christlikeness of Character.**

Now, are you getting an idea of where you should put your effort if you want to produce "fruit that will last"?

Qualities of a Christian Leader

from 4 key biblical lists

	1 Timothy 3: 1-7	1 Timothy 3: 8-13	2 Timothy 2: 22-26	Titus 1:5-9
Spiritual Obedience and Growth	not be a recent convert	keep hold of the deep truths of the faith	Flee the evil desires of youth pursue righteousness, faith, love and peace with those who call on the Lord out of a pure heart	holy, disciplined hold firmly to the trustworthy message that has been taught
How he is viewed by others	respectable, good reputation with outsiders	worthy of respect		
Personal Qualities	above reproach not given to drunkenness not violent	sincere not indulging in much wine		blameless, upright not given to drunkenness not violent not quick tempered
	not quarrelsome		Don't have anything to do with stupid arguments The Lord's servant must not quarrel	
	not a lover of money temperate, gentle self-controlled hospitable	not pursuing dishonest gain		not pursuing dishonest gain not overbearing self controlled hospitable
			kind to everyone not resentful	loves what is good
Family relationship	husband of but one wife manage his own family well with children characterised by belief and respect	husband of but one wife manage his household well Wife characterised by respect and trustworthiness		husband of but one wife with Children characterised by obedience and obedience
Gifts or Abilities	able to teach		able to teach gently instruct those who oppose	encourage others by sound doctrine refute those who oppose it

5. Encourage Firmly

"For you know that we dealt with each of you as a father deals with his own children, encouraging, comforting and urging you to live lives worthy of God who calls us into his kingdom and glory
1 Thessalonians 2: 11-12"

a) The love of a father

Previously, Paul has shown how he loves "like a mother caring for her little children". But here he shows us how vital it is to also develop a "father's love" if you want to develop a "pastors heart".

Most dads these days have no idea what is expected of them. But here Paul spells it out. A father's ministry to his children is to "encourage, comfort, and urge to live lives worthy of God". Is that what your dad did with you? I'm not sure it would accurately describe how my father treated me! As a boy, I don't ever remember my father "encouraging me" or "comforting me' or "urging me to live a life worthy of God".

But it certainly gives me a blue-print for how I am to treat my kids. I think that we fathers always have the temptation to be a little heavy handed as we "urge our kids to live a life worthy of God". But if I'm doing my fathering the way God wants me to, then as I encourage my kids to live lives that are "worthy of God", they will feel encouraged and comforted as I do that.

b) The ministry of a pastor

Do you notice something amazing about Paul's description of his own ministry amongst the Christians at Thessalonica - which he compares to the love of a father who "encourages, comforts and urges to live for God"?

If we compare this with the ministry of a New Testament prophet, you will notice some amazing similarities. It is hard to get Christians to agree on what the precise ministry of a New Testament prophet is, but there is no mistaking the **effect** that their ministry is meant to have on others.

Paul tells the Corinthians:

"But everyone who prophesies speaks to men for their strengthening, encouragement and comfort"
1 Corinthians 14:3

Strengthening (urging to live a life worthy of God), encouraging and comforting. This is the ministry of a father ... this is the ministry of a prophet ... this is the ministry of Paul as a pastor.

If you want to develop the heart of a pastor, you need to learn how to "encourage, comfort, and urge to live for God (strengthen)". It's the **balance** of these which is probably the key to growing the heart of a pastor.

It can be dangerous to get the balance wrong.

If you're encouraging and comforting students, but not "urging them to live a life worthy of God"- then they might feel very supported, but might not be held accountable to a level of godliness that will take them forward.

> I have met youth pastors who are "the nicest guys out". They love everyone, care deeply, and are wonderful people to pour your heart out to. But they don't have the courage to confront students and to raise their level of discipleship. They allow sin to fester in their students and they put up with sloppy standards from their leaders because "they don't want to upset anyone". And they want everyone to like them! They might be nice guys, but the bible does not call you to be a nice guy. It calls you to have a pastor's heart ... it calls you to have the love of a father who will urge your students to live a life that is worthy of God.

> If you do not challenge students to a high level of discipleship, then you will not produce "fruit that will last".

On the other hand, if you're "urging students to live a life worthy of God", but you're not "encouraging or comforting" them, then they might feel very challenged, but they might not feel supported enough to meet that challenge.

> I coach my son's soccer team, and I meet many other soccer coaches who are very strong on "urging their players to a better standard", but very short on "comforting and encouraging". While

they sometimes end up with teams that play well, they do not usually end up with teams that enjoy playing as a team. They have a high drop out rate. They do not produce "fruit that will last".

If you want to develop the heart of a pastor, then you need to develop a balanced ministry. Are you strong on the "urging", but run short on the "encouraging" or "comforting"? Or do you face a danger in the other direction? Check it out.

c) The ministry of encouragement

If you truly want to develop the heart of a pastor, then there is one ministry that you absolutely must master. It is the ministry of encouragement. You must learn to spur on and encourage all those around you that they might achieve their absolute best before God.

i   Encouragement can seem difficult

Encouragement is a risky business. Because by building someone else up, you are running the risk that you might feel pushed down. I believe that one of the greatest barriers to encouragement is our own personal need to feel that "I'm doing okay myself".

Here's my problem with encouragement. If I'm feeling a bit down about myself, then the last thing I feel like doing is encouraging someone else. "I'm the one who needs the encouraging!" **Yet it is rising above this that shows the true heart of a pastor!** Sure, maybe you are the one who needs encouraging, but if you are the youth pastor - if you are the youth leader - **then it needs to start with you**. Part of being a champion pastor is to be a champion encourager.

ii   Encouragement is Powerful

When I was a young boy, I learned tennis. I do not think I was very good at tennis. It was a short-lived career at the best! But I remember that one day my coach came up to me and said "Tim - you're really getting much better with your serve. I'm really proud of you".

Wow! That one word of encouragement was all I needed to try flat out to be the world's best tennis player.

In so many people that you meet in ministry, all they need from you is that one word of encouragement to lift their standards and try their heart out. There is so much power in one word of encouragement!

I was teaching a "Scripture" class in a state high school. There was one boy who was continuously badly behaved. When I corrected him, it seemed to have no result. Finally I told him a I wanted to see him at the end of class. I was determined to discipline him. But I was also determined to encourage him.

"Scott", I said "You are an amazing person . I love having you in my class. You have such a strong personality. I'm sure you have real leadership. However, there are some things that you're doing in my classroom which are simply not acceptable".

I wanted to give him a clear message that his behaviour was unacceptable. But I also wanted to affirm and strengthen him so that he would leave me encouraged.

If you want to develop the heart of a pastor ... if you want to show the love of a father ... if you want to produce fruit that will last, then you must learn to be a champion encourager.

iii Encouragement is central

This is especially true with your fellow leaders.

Build them up, strengthen them, encourage them so that they will fly far past you and beyond you. I want my leaders to be better than me, and I am delighted to be one of the encouragers that help them to leave me in their wake.

One of those people that I strived to encourage was John Warren. John worked as an intern with me, and I believe that God is now preparing him to impact this world in a big way. I asked each person on my team to come up with a personal mission statement

- something that would drive them through life and stand behind everything they would achieve.

Here is John's personal mission statement. I reckon it is a beauty,

> *"To build something big for God, by building big people around me."*

Can you see how encouragement is woven into his very mission statement? The **way** he will build something big for God, is by sowing into, building up, strengthening and encouraging those whom God has placed around him.

I would love for you to have a personal mission statement that reflected the fact that you were going to be a life-long encourager.

Try to encourage every one of your leaders this week. Encourage every one of your students every time you see them. Encourage everyone on e-mail or ICQ. Encourage each of your friends. Encourage your family members. Try and make a difference to every person you meet. You will be amazed by the ministry that you will unleash!

Learn to be an encourager. Learn to develop a pastor's heart. Learn to produce "fruit that will last".

SECTION 3

How to Grow A Plan That Will Last

Chapter 7
Developing a Biblical Plan

1. The Road to Nowhere

"Let's get our youth ministry back on its feet again!"
"Sure thing! What'll we do?"
"Dunno. Let's ask the kids."
"All they ever want is outings"
"Well, we can have some of those, but we probably ought to have some bible studies as well"
"Okay, as long as they're interesting"
"What about some singing?"
"Yeah – lets do some of that as well"
"As long as the kids come"
"As long as they enjoy it"

As long as the kids come.
As long as they enjoy it.

These are the unwritten rules that lie behind the vast majority of youth ministries that operate out of local churches around the world.

As long as the kids come.
As long as they enjoy it.

And I've seen lots of youth programmes that have stacks of kids coming, and the kids seem to enjoy it. Based on the above 2 guidelines, you would have to conclude that these youth groups are "successful"

As long as the kids come.
As long as they enjoy it.

If this is your only plan, you will never build "fruit that will last". You will never really know whether your group is "successful" or not. You will never know whether you've achieved the things that are really worth achieving..

As long as the kids come.
As long as they enjoy it.
This is the road to nowhere.

2. The Questions that Bring Real Success

If you're going to build a "successful" youth ministry; if you're going to develop a ministry that has lasting impact, you need to be able to answer the following questions:

- What are you meant to do in your youth ministry?

- Why do you do what you do?

- How can you be the most effective in what you do?

- How do you measure or evaluate what you do?

- ARE YOU ACTUALLY ACCOMPLISHING THE THINGS THAT GOD WANTS YOU TO DO?

Every one of us wants to be successful. We all want to have a youth ministry that's successful. But how do we work out what "success" really means?

Try this for a working definition:

> *"Success is when you achieve the things that are really worthwhile achieving"*

Here's why it really matters to have a plan – a good plan – a biblical plan.

If you haven't worked out what God really wants you to achieve in your local youth ministry, you will never know whether you are being successful or not!

If you haven't worked out from the bible what it is that God wants you to achieve in your youth ministry, then it is unlikely your ministry - no matter how "successful" looking it is - **will be of any value on God's kingdom!**

3. Five Steps to a Youth Ministry That Goes Nowhere

Step 1 – Start with your own ideas

Start with your own ideas and plans. All those dreams you've ever had of having a world-shattering youth ministry, just start without checking them out. A youth ministry that goes nowhere will always starts with **you and your ideas.** It will always be "me-centred".

This may sound a little harsh, but it will always result in the following statement. See if it sounds familiar.

> *"We can help solve the problems of youth"*

As soon as you come up with a statement that it is somehow up to us to solve the problems of youth, you know that you're starting on a plan that revolves around you, and not around God.

Step 2 – Try to Meet Everybody's Expectations

Once you have established that you can solve the problems of youth, you will need to find out what those problems are. You will try and discover the "needs" of your youth. And you will discover that they need fun, and friendship and acceptance and a whole host of things that flow from that.

But of course, your youth aren't the only ones with needs. They have parents who have needs and expectations as well. They want somewhere "nice" for their teenager to attend. So you want to have a youth programme that is outrageous enough to attract the teenagers, but sedate enough to please their parents.

Your pastor will have expectations as well. He wants to attract families to his church. A vibrant youth ministry is absolutely necessary. So it better be "family friendly" - and those kids better keep quiet during his sermons!

Your board of elders or deacons or parish councillors have needs and expectations as well. They don't want your youth group to wreck the church hall, or leave it untidy for Sunday School, or create too much noise and annoy the neighbours. But they do want you to be big – and to grow. They need to produce annual statistics for their church, and it always looks good when the youth ministry is growing!

And of course, you yourself have needs and expectations. You want to be successful; you want to make a mark on the world. It's nice to be needed and loved and to have teenagers who will pour out their hearts to you. So you want a ministry that will not only look attractive, but also one that you will feel good about as well.

Step 3 – Make your Goal to keep everybody happy

Keep those kids coming. Make sure they're enjoying themselves. If they stop coming, change the programme. Keep those parents happy. Make sure it's a nice "safe" place that they can send little Johnny to.

Keep your pastor happy. He loves to see those kids in church – but could you please keep them quiet? They are so restless! Stick your leaders in with them. Tell them to be quiet. SShhhh!!!

Keep those deacon/elders/parish councillors happy. Don't have messy games; don't wreck the hall; keep everything tidy and make sure your numbers are getting bigger and bigger and bigger.

And of course make sure you're feeling good about all this. Centre it around yourself. Make yourself indispensable. Make sure you're needed. And make sure you're loved. Don't make any decisions that would get the kids offside.

Make sure that the **goal** of your ministry is to meet everybody's needs and keep everybody happy.

> Back in the early days of Crossfire, we reached a crisis point. We had a very "activity based" programme. We had started with all the wrong questions. We didn't have a biblical plan. We were on the road to nowhere.

But we looked successful. We had big numbers. Lots of activity. We had a Year 7 group with about 70 in it. We had a year 8 group with about 80 in it. But each year we had a problem with Year 9. It would start the year with 80-90 students attending, and by the half-way point, it would drop to 30-40.

I challenged my leaders as to whether we could hold onto these kids. We put **so** much effort into our Year 9 ministry. We did everything we could think of. Better games. More outings. More supervision. We looked after the Year 9 drunks who showed up. We tolerated the disruptive kids. We increased our leadership resources.

And can I say we did it? Through an enormous amount of effort we held onto our Year 9 numbers right throughout the year!

Was it worth it? **Absolutely not.** Yes, we held onto the students until the end of the year, but we lost them at the beginning of Year 10 the next year. Our leaders were working so hard at "keeping the kids coming", they had no energy left to look after the students who were responding. My leaders were exhausted. Some left. Very few students became Christians. Very few students grew as Christians.

There was nothing wrong with our passion. There was nothing wrong with our enthusiasm. But we were staring at the wrong place. We did not have a biblical plan.

We were on the road to nowhere.

Step 4 – Have a programme that will achieve your goal

If your goal is to try and meet everyone's needs, and to keep everybody happy, you will have a frantic programme that races around trying to please everyone. Kids are stopping coming? Tone down the bible studies – have more outings. Parents are getting worried? Use tighter discipline and keep away those "unchurched" kids. Can't find enough leaders? Drop your standards and take anyone who'll volunteer.

Keep those kids coming. Keep them enjoying it. Placate those parents. Please your pastor. Live up to the expectations of your deacons.

You'll have a frantic programme. You might even have a "great" programme. But you will achieve very little. And you'll be exhausted.

Step 5 – The Natural Result – Burn Out

Why do so many volunteer youth leaders last less than a year? Why do so many Youth Pastors give up inside three years? Because if you're trying to meet everyone's needs – if you're trying to keep everyone happy – if you're racing around attempting to beef up a programme that will keep those kids coming, and keep them happy – and keep everybody else happy at the same time – you will be exhausted. You will be tired. You will be discouraged. You will burn out. You will give up.

You know the other problem? You are more likely to be unfaithful.

> When I am tired – when I am pushing too hard – when I feel wrung out - I am far more likely to stray into temptation and sin. Because when I'm feeling "bad"- I desperately want to feel "good". I will look for a shortcut to feeling "good". And usually those shortcuts will involve sin.

So many youth leaders drop out from youth ministry – not because they didn't have the passion – not because they didn't have the ability – but because they got exhausted – and their own sin let them down.

If this is starting to happen to you – STOP.

There is another way.

4. Five Steps to growing a Biblical Plan

Step 1 – Discover God's ideas and Plans

Rather than starting with "what I can do for youth"; rather than sitting down and trying to work out a master plan to "do something for young people"; start by working out what God's ideas are. He has a whole book full of his thoughts and ideas.

You can know what he wants. He has written it in the bible, and given you his Spirit so that you might understand it. If you want to know what God would want to do for the young people in your area, then continue on with a life that is immersed in prayer and God's word. Stay vitally united to Jesus. All that stuff that was in the last section "Grow a heart that will last" – it really matters!

What does God want you to achieve with the young people at your church? It's a good starting point. And his word will give you the answers.

Step 2 – Discover the Real Needs of Youth

When you spend time in God's word, you will have no doubt as to what the **real** needs of youth are. And this is where your focus will be. Sure - they have many surface needs (fun, acceptance, love, activities etc.), but if you want to have a **real** ministry with them, you need to meet their **real** needs. If you want to have a **lasting** ministry, you need to address their **lasting** needs.

What are the real needs of youth? God's word will spell them out for you.

They need to be saved. They need to be filled with God's Spirit. They need to be built as strong disciples. They need to be equipped as effective disciple-makers. They need to worship the one true and living God. They need to develop a Christlike character. They need to show God's love to the world. They need to develop a heart for the poor. They need to develop a passion for their unsaved friends. They need to discover and action their spiritual gifts. They need to serve the body of Christ. They need to be raised as leaders to plant and spearhead ministries around this planet. They need ...

When you look into God's word, you will discover the real needs of youth.

Step 3 – Establish Biblical Goals

When you discover from God's word the real needs of youth, then you will end up with goals that will help meet those needs, You will end up with biblical goals ... like evangelism ... discipleship ... accountability ... shepherding ... equipping ...

These will be the benchmarks that you will measure your youth ministry against. These are the markers that will keep you on track. These will be the indicators of whether you really are achieving the things that God wants you to achieve.

Step 4 – Have a programme that will achieve your Biblical Goals

Your programme is only a **temporary, flexible** expression of the best way to achieve your biblical goals. Your biblical goals will never change, but your programme might change often – depending on whether it is effectively meeting your biblical criteria.

Section 4 of this book "How to grow a Ministry that will Last" will go into detail about what your programme might look like. But here is the key question.

"What methods does God say will achieve his biblical goals?"

An amazing question. But here's what's more amazing. **God provides his answers in his book!** If you're trying to look for programme ideas, God actually spells out the **methods** that will achieve his biblical **goals.**

And you thought youth ministry was going to be hard! God's done all the difficult bits for you already!

More about all this later!

Step 5 – The Natural Result – Evaluation and Revision

If you immerse your life in God's word and prayer; if you discover the real needs of youth – if you establish biblical goals, and a programme which reflects all that ... the natural result will be regular evaluation, and regular revision.

You will learn to ask questions like:

- Are we really achieving what God wants us to achieve?
- Is what we're doing the **best** way to achieve our biblical goals?
- Is there a more effective way to achieve what God wants us to achieve?

- What do we need to do differently this year because the world is a different place this year?

If you look at Crossfire, the youth ministry at our church, you will see it is constantly changing. Our biblical goals remain the same, but the **programme** – the way we achieve those biblical goals – changes from year to year. That is because we are constantly evaluating, and constantly revising our programme to try and have the maximum impact. The world is different from what is was 5 years ago. Kids are different from what they were a few years ago. You get a particular age group of students who seem to have a "group" personality" that is far different from the year ahead of them – or the year behind them. The numbers you have in a particular age group will change the way you deliver your programme. How many leaders you have will help determine what "package" you come up with. What facilities you have will have an influence on what you do.

We have not changed our biblical goals. But in my 12 years at our church as youth pastor, we have only ever had 2 years in a row where our programme was the same. Every year, there are reasons to re-evaluate what we're doing, and to try more effective ways of achieving our biblical goals.

Leaders who are not changing are leaders who are not learning and growing.

5. Four Results of having a Biblical Plan

1. A Biblical Plan establishes a direction

It is essential that your youth ministry knows where it is going. If your youth ministry has a biblical plan (if you know "why" you do what you do), then your youth ministry has a purpose. I can assure you, if you don't know where you're going, it's very unlikely you will get there!

If you aim at nothing, then you're sure to hit it!

A biblical plan will shape and select the ministry choices and options that every youth ministry faces so you can accomplish your biblical goals. A biblical plan will determine which activities you decide to do, and which you decide to do without. It will help you choose which programmes are right for your group, and which ones are not.

Every week I have stacks of Christ-honouring ministries from around the planet who send me literature, because they are convinced that our youth ministry should join in what they are doing. Most of these are good things. But we cannot do everything. Our biblical plan helps us to make wise decisions as to what will help us to achieve the goals that we believe God has placed before us.

A biblical plan will shape the direction of a youth ministry so that the ministry as a whole will produce a product: it will train mature disciples and disciple-makers as the future leaders of the church. If that is one of you end goals, you need a biblical plan to help get you there.

2. A biblical plan defines success

A biblical plan will help you measure true success. Numbers, fun, activity and excitement (as measures of success) will give way to biblical fruit, changed character, and lives that endure. When you know what your plan is, you know whether you are on track. You know if you will get there. You know whether you are being "successful" at what you set out to achieve

The true test of a youth ministry is to evaluate whether those teenagers still stand for Christ (and live totally for him) when they get out on their own.

3. A biblical plan lays a foundation

A biblical plan (once established) will stand longer than the typical youth worker or volunteer leader. A biblical philosophy will lay a foundation that other workers can build on. It will prevent a youth ministry from depending merely on one person.

If your plan is biblical, and your plan is a good plan, it will save your youth ministry from simply going along with the latest trends, or slavishly following the advice from the latest guest speaker or youth ministry book. (even great books like this one!)

4. A biblical plan communicates effectively

A biblical plan for youth ministry (once established and written) will communicate effectively to your own leaders as to "where the whole thing is going". This will make it much easier for your own leaders to have an effective ministry with you. Your biblical plan will also communicate effectively to your pastor, to other ministries, to other pastoral staff, to wardens, parish councillors, youth leaders, parents etc. what is going on in the programme and what your youth ministry is trying to accomplish (and why it cannot do everything!)

You will be amazed how accepting your fiercest critics can be when they see that what you are doing is attempting to follow an established biblical plan.

> Shortly after we made the change from being an "activity-centred" youth ministry to a "disciple-making" youth ministry, a concerned church parent approached me.
>
> *"My little Johnny doesn't like coming to Crossfire any more. He says it's too "bible-y" He says it's too boring. Perhaps if you have some more outings, he might be more interested in coming along."*
>
> My heart goes out to a parent like this. Every Christian parent wants to have their child plugged in to their church's youth ministry. It must be so distressing when your child says to you "I don't want to go any more".
>
> But because we have a written biblical plan, I didn't just say *"Sure, we'll change the programme for you"*. I handed them a copy of our biblical plan and said *"I'm genuinely sorry that little Johnny is not ready yet for what we're doing at Crossfire. But this document will explain why we are doing things this way. I will really pray that Johnny progresses in his spiritual understanding so he will be ready for what we're doing".*

This parent was able to accept why we were doing what we were doing because we had a biblical plan. We did not abandon our plan simply because one person wasn't fitting in with it. We prayed for Johnny, and about a year later he gave his life to Christ, and joined one of our discipleship groups,

Do you see how vital it is to have a biblical plan for your youth ministry?

But how do you do it?

Read on!

Chapter 8
The "One Purpose" of Youth Ministry

1. 'Why does your youth ministry exist?'

The first step to working out a biblical plan for your youth ministry, is to determine your **purpose**. That is, why does your youth ministry exist? Why is it there in the first place? What is the one sole reason why it matters that your youth ministry is there? Or more importantly ... "Why does God want you to have a youth ministry at your local church?"

This is a question that rarely gets asked. "Why have a youth ministry?" Ask that of any local group of youth leaders, and they will probably have some interesting answers.

> *"Because we've always had a youth ministry"*

> *"Every good church has a youth ministry"*

> (I think the above rule must exist. I don't know where it's written down, but I'm sure everyone in the world believes it. If you don't believe me, try closing down the youth ministry at your church and see what happens!)

Now I know that you're a cluey, biblical thinking youth pastor, and you wouldn't come up with an answer as simplistic as those above. I'm sure you'd come up with something far more solid.

But the question still needs to be asked

"Why **does** your youth ministry exist?"

> *"To reach kids for Christ"*

> *"To impact our local youth community"*

"To grow the church of tomorrow"

"For evangelism, discipleship, worship, fellowship and equipping"

Hey! All these are great things. But can I make a bold suggestion?

Not one of these is the biblical purpose as to why your youth ministry exists!

You've missed a step. You've gone straight onto the **tasks** that you should be doing. You've leapt ahead to the **mission** you should be undertaking. You've jumped into the sort of **activities** you should be running. **But you have skipped over the one underlying purpose that governs everything!**

2. Don't confuse 'purpose' with 'mission'

Right now you could write down a list of good biblical things you should be doing in your youth ministry

- reaching the lost
- building up young disciples
- creating a biblical community
- making a stand against social injustice
- encouraging a community of prayer
- teaching teenagers to worship
- equipping young people of ministry
- etc. etc. etc.

Now all these things are biblical things. All these things are good things. But you can't do all of these all the time at 100% effort. You can't focus on everything!

So how do you know where to focus? **That's where you need to know your purpose.**

If you haven't worked out your one biblical purpose, your ministry will end up following the latest trend or focussing where the most pressure is.

Someone will produce a great book on prayer – and so that's where your youth ministry will head!

"We've got to pray! And pray more"
"Shouldn't we study the bible sometimes?"
"No - no use getting to the bible unless we've built a big enough prayer base"

Then you go to a conference on "Worship" and you come back all fired up.

"We've got to teach our young people to worship. They need to know how to praise God! That's our most central thing! Where are those musicians?"
"Shouldn't we go out and evangelise?
"No – people will be brought to Jesus through worship"

And so the cycle goes one. One year the focus is "discipleship". One month the focus is "mission". At another stage the youth ministry goes totally into "ministry training". All of these are good things, but with no overall purpose guiding them, your youth ministry can lurch from one good focus to another **and never produce fruit that will last**.

I remember catching up with a Children's Pastor from a church down the road. He was looking a little exasperated.

"What's up?"
"I just want to reach kids for Christ, and I get blocked with everything I try to do"

He went on to explain that they had started a new Children's Club at his church, and he had asked the local public school whether he could do a lunch-time "presentation" to advertise his new children's club. Permission was granted and he showed up and set up his ministry stand.

But what he failed to realise was that Christians from other churches in the area had had a ministry at that school ever since it opened. They came down each week, and taught "Scripture" classes to almost every child in the school. Theirs was a faithful and long -term ministry. Unfortunately, he did not consult with these representatives from other churches. None of them knew he was there. None of them knew who he was. None of them knew what church he was from.

There was a little bit of uneasiness at the school because of this lack of communication. He felt a bit rejected and isolated. His grand plans for his children's club had had a small setback.

"Did you ever think of contacting the Christians from the other churches and working in partnership with them?" I innocently asked.
"But what if they got in my way? I just want to reach kids for Christ.
"I imagine that they want to reach kids for Christ as well".
"But they might have blocked my plans. I just want to reach kids for Christ".

You can tell by his words what he thought his purpose was. "To reach kids for Christ" A hugely commendable idea!

But I believe he has missed a step. If he had got his purpose right it would've affected the **way** he reached kids for Christ. He could've avoided the friction with the Christians from the other churches.

So ... what was the step he'd missed?

3. Your One Central Purpose

a) Your purpose governs everything you do

When you work out your biblical purpose, that becomes the "controller" of everything you do. Your purpose will not only decide **what** you do, but also **how** you do it.

Wouldn't it be great to have **one purpose** for your youth ministry so that you could know whether you were on track at any given moment?

At Crossfire, we have developed one over-arching purpose that guides and steers everything we do. One "grid" that we can pass everything through to determine whether that is the right thing to do. One question which we can ask of every suggestion, ministry opportunity, activity or plan so that we know we are heading in the direction that God wants us to.

One purpose.

One over-arching guideline for everything.

Are you ready?

b) Our purpose for Crossfire

Here is our purpose statement. It is expressed in a question and answer form. This is expected to be memorised and actualised by every student and every adult on our ministry team.

"Why does Crossfire exist?"

"We exist to give huge honour to our awesome God."

Aarrgghh!! You shelled out all your money for this book, and you were expecting something brand new and earth shattering, and all you got was ...

"We exist to give huge honour to our awesome God."

Our purpose is to glorify God. Our purpose is to honour God. Our aim is that everything we do in our youth ministry will bring honour to God. Our ideal is that nothing we do in our youth ministry will dishonour God.

Can you notice at this point that we have said nothing about our mission or the tasks that we are meant to do? Our central purpose is not to reach kids for Christ, or build strong disciples, or to impact the world ... all these are vital ... and all these are in the next step ... but the central reason that there is a youth ministry at St. Paul's Castle Hill NSW Australia is so that God will be honoured. We believe that more glory and honour will be given to God because we exist, than if we didn't exist.

How did we end up with that purpose?

It's the purpose that God gave us!

c) So what is "God's Glory"?

"Glory" is one of those difficult words to define. It's not the sort of word that we tend to use in our day to day conversations. It comes from the Hebrew word meaning "heaviness, weight, or worthiness". It is used by people to describe their wealth, splendour or reputation. God's glory is where God's very nature is revealed - when it can be shown, seen, experienced. – first hand and unimpeded. Raw and exposed before you. God's glory is when you see God first hand at his absolute best!

I grew up at Brookvale, a middle to working class suburb of Sydney. Down the road was Brookvale Oval, the home of the mighty Manly Warringah Sea Eagles. They were the local Rugby League team, and as a youngster I would go down and watch my heroes play.

When do you see the "glory" of Manly-Warringah? Not when they're on a huge losing streak! You see their "glory" – you see them at their best – when at the end of a long winning streak they win the premiership and are crowned at the Rugby League champions of Australia.

So too, you see God's glory when you see his raw power and might is displayed before you.

So where do you see this?

4. Jesus' Purpose was to show God's glory

God's glory is mainly displayed in Jesus.

a) His whole life

"The Word became flesh and made his dwelling among us. We have seen his glory, the glory of the One and Only, who came from the Father, full of grace and truth."
John 1:14

"The Son is the radiance of God's glory and the exact representation of his being, sustaining all things by his powerful word"
Hebrews 1:3a

Jesus spends his whole life pursuing God's glory. Just before he dies, as he talks with his Father in the garden, he sums up his life in these words:

"I have brought you glory on earth by completing the work you gave me to do.
John 17:4

As you look through the life of Jesus, you see that at every point, he is relentless in displaying the glory of God.

b) His Miracles

When Jesus performs his miracles, he reveals God's glory and power.

"This, the first of his miraculous signs, Jesus performed at Cana in Galilee. He thus revealed his glory, and his disciples put their faith in him.
John 2:11

c) His Death

The central point where Jesus shows God's glory is when he dies on the cross.

"Now my heart is troubled, and what shall I say? `Father, save me from this hour'? No, it was for this very reason I came to this hour. Father, glorify your name!" Then a voice came from heaven, "I have glorified it, and will glorify it again."
John 12:27-28

d) His exaltation

Certainly as he was raised from death and exalted to heaven, he displayed the glory and majesty of God.

He appeared in a body, was vindicated by the Spirit, was seen by angels, was preached among the nations, was believed on in the world, was taken up in glory.
1 Timothy 3:16

e) His return

Jesus will display God's glory when he returns!

> *"When the Son of Man comes in his glory, and all the angels with him,*
> *he will sit on his throne in heavenly glory".*
> **Matthew 25:31**

Do you get the picture? This is just a small example of how Jesus absolutely dedicated himself to one purpose in his life – that at every point he would bring glory to his father God.

So ... if Jesus spent his life pursuing God's glory, guess what the purpose for your life is meant to be?

5. Your Purpose is to show God's glory

The overall aim for any individual - or for any ministry - is to glorify God.. We were created for the purpose of pursuing God's glory, revealing God's glory, and bringing honour to his name. This verse from Isaiah tells us why each one of us was made.

> *"everyone who is called by my name,* **whom I created for my glory**,
> *whom I formed and made."*
> **Isaiah 43:7**

The psalms are full of encouragement that the one purpose we exist is to bring honour and glory to our God.

> *Psalm 29:1-2, 85:9, 115:1*

That gives you a huge incentive for your own life. Your were created so that God would be glorified! Wow! What a huge purpose for any individual! And what a huge purpose for any ministry!

6. How do you glorify God?

So if you're created to bring glory to God, how do you go about achieving that?

a) Aim your whole life at glorifying God

> *So whether you eat or drink or whatever you do, do it all for the glory*
> *of God.*
> **1 Corinthians 10:31**

If you have your whole life lined up with "God's Glory" as your target, then you'll find that lots of things you do on the way will also bring honour to God. It's the way you will head with everything. Paul says to the Corinthians "In everything you do – do it all for the glory of God". God says to you "Likewise".

b) Keep submitting to Jesus as Lord

> *"that at the name of Jesus every knee should bow, in heaven and on earth and under the earth, and every tongue confess that Jesus Christ is Lord, to the glory of God the Father".*
> ### *Philippians 2:10-11*

Every time someone bows their knee before Jesus; every time someone confesses that Jesus is their Lord - God is honoured. Because He is the one who has placed Jesus there as Lord! So when we treat Jesus as Lord, God gets the glory!

God is honoured every time a person turns to Christ. God is honoured every time that you bring an area of your life under the lordship of Jesus. On the other hand, God is dishonoured every time you refuse to bow to Jesus' lordship in some area of your life.

c) Confess your sin.

Every time you acknowledge your sin, and bring it before God, he is glorified.

During the Battle of Jericho, one of God's soldiers named Achan sinned against God. He took some things which God had specifically told him not to take. Because of this sin, the mighty army of God is defeated the next day when they attempt to overtake the little town of Ai. Eventually God points out to Joshua that Achan is the problem – it is his sin which has brought the whole community down.

Achan doesn't own up to his sin. So eventually Joshua says to him

> *"My son, give glory to the LORD, the God of Israel, and give him the praise. Tell me what you have done; do not hide it from me."*
> ### *Joshua 7:19*

God is honoured when you confess your sin. On the other hand, God is dishonoured when you hang onto your sin. Sin shows that you are falling short of God's glory.

> *"for all have sinned and fall short of the glory of God,"*
> **Romans 3:23**

d) Trust God's Promises

Abraham was kinda old. He had a promise from God that he would have a child. Humanly speaking it seemed impossible. And yet he trusted God's promise.

> *"Yet he did not waver through unbelief regarding the promise of God, but was strengthened in his faith and gave glory to God,"*
> **Romans 4:20**

Every time you trust one of God's promises – and put your life on the line because of it – God is glorified. On the other hand, every time you doubt one of God's promises – and don't trust him, honour and glory is taken away from God.

e) This will all affect your ministry

Why does it matter that you make sure that you have a life that brings honour to God?

Because if your life isn't bringing glory to God, your ministry never will!

Do you want to have a ministry that glorifies God? Good! Then make sure that your life is doing the same!

7. So, the purpose for your youth ministry...

I want you to work out that you will have one over-arching purpose for your youth ministry. Before you get onto saving the world or increasing your numbers or anything else, will you pause for a moment and determine before God what the overall biblical purpose of your ministry will be?

I can assure you, your youth ministry exists so that God will be glorified. Nothing more, nothing less. This is the one "filter" that you can run everything through. This is the one question you can ask of any proposal, any plan, any idea, any activity any ministry that your youth group is planning. "Will this glorify God?" This will determine not only **what** you do, but **how** you do it.

If there's a way of bringing kids to Christ (sounds like a good idea!) but the **method** wouldn't honour God, then don't do it that way! If your purpose is to glorify God, then everything you do will be changed by that single purpose.

One of the key changes for us at Crossfire was to realise what our central purpose was. Before we learnt about "glorifying God", we just ploughed ahead reaching kids, discipling kids, and all those good things. But there was no purpose behind it. There was no "control" behind it. There was no direction behind it. Discovering a biblical purpose has absolutely reshaped our ministry, and I want to challenge you to allow it to reshape yours as well.

When we show the fruit of ministry - when we bear "fruit that will last", God is glorified. There can be no higher purpose for your ministry.

> *"This is to my Father's glory, that you bear much fruit, showing yourselves to be my disciples."*
> **John 15:8**
>
> *"You did not choose me, but I chose you and appointed you to go and bear fruit - fruit that will last"*
> **John 15:16**

Now that you have established your biblical **purpose**, you know why your youth ministry exists.

But how do you work out what you're meant to do?

How do you determine your biblical **mission**?

Read on!

Chapter 9
The "One Mission" of Youth Ministry

1. So what's your youth ministry meant to DO?

Okay! So you worked out your purpose! You know **why** your youth ministry exists. You are there so that God is honoured and glorified. You're going to make sure that everything you do in your own life – and everything that happens in your youth ministry – will glorify God.

So – what is it that you're actually meant to achieve? What task are you meant to accomplish in the youth ministry at your local church? What is the one job – the one end product – the main thing that you will actually do so that God will be glorified through your ministry?

And how do you know when you're doing it right? When you get to the end of a year, how will you assess whether you have done what God wanted you to do?

If discovering our biblical purpose (why we exist - to glorify God) was the first turning point for Crossfire, then discovering our biblical mission (what God wants us to actually do) was the second. Knowing that Jesus has left us one over-arching mission – one clear objective – one task that ultimately brings him the greatest glory – has unleashed us and empowered us in an amazing way. Because I know that Jesus has left **one mission** for our youth ministry, I feel so unburdened. I am no longer weighed down with the feeling that we have to do "everything". It's amazingly refreshing to know that there's only one thing that God wants us to do.

One mission.

One task.

One "end product" that we're looking for

This is the second of the "question and answer" statements that we expect every student and every adult on our Crossfire ministry team to memorise

---

"What Does God Want Us To Achieve?"

**"We will impact the world for Christ
by empowering students to be
passionate disciples of Christ"**

---

2. The One Mission that Jesus Left For Us

a) To Make Disciples ...

You see, our statement that answers the question "What Does God Want Us To Achieve?" is simply our local expression of the one command – the one mission – that Jesus left for his church to accomplish.

> *"All authority in heaven and on earth has been given to me. Therefore go and make disciples of all nations, baptising them in the name of the Father and of the Son and of the Holy Spirit, and teaching them to obey everything I have commanded you. And surely I am with you always, to the very end of the age."*
> **Matthew 28:18-20**

I never studied New Testament Greek. I rely on the English translators to give me an accurate picture of what God's word says. But I know enough people who did study New Testament Greek to understand that the one command in Jesus' Great Commission is "make disciples". That is the one over-riding command, and the parts of it ("go", "baptise" , "teach") are explanations of how that is to occur.

One mission.

One task.

One "end product" that we're looking for.

> *"to make disciples of all nations"*

b) " ... of all nations"

In a moment I want to talk about what "making disciples" actually means, but just before we do, can I point out 3 little words that I overlooked the first time I worked this through?

Jesus' command for his church:

*"to make disciples of **all nations**"*

When I first tried to work through a "Mission Statement" for Crossfire, it only had 3 words: "To make disciples". That is, I only had a **local** vision for what we could achieve. Sure – I knew that God's vision was worldwide – I supported those missionaries who went overseas to do their bit – but my own vision was limited. I guess I had worked out that my job in this "worldwide" mission was simply to make disciples in my small patch – my local area. As long as lots of other people were all faithfully working "their small patch" somewhere else in the world – then the whole world would be reached.

But God showed me that I had limited vision. Our mission wasn't "to make disciples" but "to make disciples **of all nations**". I had unwittingly established a limited vision for Crossfire. We were only intent on making disciples. We had not yet enlarged our vision to include "all nations".

When this first hit me, I said "Lord, but how?" How could our little youth ministry possibly impact "all nations"? We had no plan ... no programme ... no personnel ... no resources ... no idea on how we could start to change the destiny of other nations by growing disciples worldwide.

But I was convicted by God that he **wanted** us to think "worldwide" as we set out on our mission of making disciples. I didn't know "how" – all I knew was – God wanted Crossfire to "make disciples **of all nations**".

Can I challenge your youth ministry to have the same worldwide focus?

Even though we didn't know "how" or "when" or anything else, we started talking and thinking and acting like we were going to have a worldwide impact. In our prayers we started praying that we could make disciples in all the world. In the way we talked about our ministry and inspired and challenged each other, we started talking like we could make an impact on the world. As I trained young men and women to become disciples, I filled them with a vision that God could use them to change nations.

Slowly, the way we started to think – and speak – and act – changed. Our vision was becoming bigger. And as our vision enlarged, so did our ministry. I still don't know the final details of "how" we will impact the world – but let me point out one major point I have discovered already: **when we enlarged our vision to become a worldwide ministry, our local ministry got better!**

Did you catch that? When we enlarged our vision to become a worldwide ministry, our local ministry got better! Don't be scared to paint a big vision of what is possible through your ministry. We have a God who is a very "big vision" God. And he has left us a very "big vision" ministry – to make disciples of all nations. Don't just concentrate on your own turf and leave it up to the missionary organisations to touch the rest of the world. Start praying that God will use your ministry to impact and change nations!

And stand back and watch the results!

Already God is starting to answer our prayers – in small ways. Already I have had the privilege of sharing with some pastors who have come from other countries. I have been enabled to speak at conferences which have touched the lives of christians from overseas. Even in writing this book, some of our "worldwide" aim will, help to be fulfilled. (If you're reading this book in any other country than Australia, then you are part of the answer to our prayers!) We are now on board with "Evangelism Explosion" and we are looking for the opportunity to take some of our trained high-schoolers overseas to bless and encourage ministry training in another nation.

But I believe that the major "worldwide" impact that we will have is that the students whom we are training to be disciples will be moved by God to have an impact among the nations. As we train disciples here at St. Paul's, it is with the prayer and the expectation and the hope and the vision that they will be used by God to impact this world for him.

That's why our mission statement reads:

"What Does God Want Us To Achieve?"

**"We will impact the world for Christ
by empowering students to be
passionate disciples of Christ"**

3. The Myth of having a Department of Discipleship

Let me tell you how we used to try and do it. This is a model that I see repeated in various forms in many many churches – and in many, many youth ministries. It's not a wrong model, but I'm not sure it's the best way to "make disciples".

It goes something like this. "Discipleship" is one of the "sections" in your ministry. It's the bit that's got to do with "what do we do with people once they've made a commitment to follow Jesus".

In it's simplest form it looks like Figure 9.1

This model sees ministry in "compartments". This is the simplest "2-step" model around. Evangelism is the first step; Discipleship is the second step. There are of course, more complex "3-step" "4-step" etc variations that you can have.

And let me just say that these are good and Godly things. You certainly need to have different ministries for those who are just seeking Jesus, and those who are built up in their faith.

However, I think the focus on "making disciples" gets a bit lost in here.

Evangelism	Discipleship
The ministry we have to people before they become Christians	The ministry we have to people after they become Christians.

Figure 9.1

In the early days of our youth ministry, we followed this model. We had Friday Night Youth groups which were evangelistic, and if a student committed his life to Jesus there, we would plug him in to a completely separate ministry – with a completely separate leadership team – where he would be "discipled" – taught the bible, challenged to Christlikeness etc. etc.

95

I used to work in a church which modelled this division in its staff. We had a "Minister for Evangelism", and a "Minister for Discipleship". Each knew his job. The "Minister for Evangelism" would work at devising programmes to reach out to non-Christians, and looking at ways of equipping Christians to share the gospel. The "Minister for Discipleship" made sure there were bible study groups for the Christians, and teaching on a variety of topics. to produce growth in the lives of individual Christians.

All these are great things. All these are biblical things. But where do we "make disciples"? Is it in "evangelism" – or "discipleship"? The word "discipleship" probably gives the clue as to where this model thinks it lies. In "evangelism" we make "converts"; in "discipleship" we make "disciples".

But does this really reflect the biblical model? Does this reflect Jesus' command? Does it emphasise what "making disciples" is all about? **Does it produce world-changing disciples? Does it bear "fruit that will last?"**

4. Jesus' Model of Discipleship

When I think about Jesus' ministry, I tend to picture him with the crowds. I can visualise him crying out as he preaches to the multitudes in the Sermon on the Mount. I can see him standing before the 5000+ as he multiplies the loaves and fishes. I can easily imagine the crowds swarming around as he miraculously brings God's healing I can even picture the angry crowd jeering as Jesus is condemned to death. Most youth pastors look at these vivid, dynamic pictures and think "Yes, Lord Give me a ministry like that!" (with the exception, perhaps, of being put to death at the end of it!)

But if you look at Jesus' 3 years of ministry, he uniquely spent it with 12 men. Yes, he ministered to the crowds, but his overwhelming investment of time was with just 12 men. He wasn't interested in merely having a spectacular ministry for 3 years and then disappearing. (Youth Pastors would never do that, would they?) He was looking to usher in a kingdom. He was seeking to build disciples. He spend his time with 12 imperfect, inadequate men so that he might "make disciples of all nations". He was setting up a plan that would multiply his disciples throughout the planet.

He wanted his kingdom to not just be confined to Israel, but to reach Judea, Samaria, and the ends of the earth (even Australia!) He didn't want to just attract a crowd, and then leave them leaderless, to wilt on the vine. He had a disciple-making strategy. He wanted to build "fruit that would last".

Jesus brought people to himself, that he might build them up, and then send them out.

> *"He appointed twelve–designating them apostles– that they might be with him and that he might send them out to preach ..."*
> **Mark 3:14**

Do you see the strategy?

a) He brought a small number to himself – *"He appointed twelve– designating them apostles"*

b) He built them up – by investing time in them - *"that they might be with him"*

c) Then he sent them out *"and that he might send them out to preach ..."*

So ... which bit is the "disciple-making" bit? The "bringing in", the "building up" or the "sending out"?

The whole lot!

Jesus made disciples by bringing a small number of people to himself, building them up, and then sending them out to do the same for others.

"Discipleship" is therefore not a "section" in your programme and it is not primarily something you teach in a course.

True Discipleship is when a learning and maturing disciple invests his time in someone else's life, helps bring them to maturity in Christ; sows God's word into them; implants in them a passion for ministry, and equips them to go out and make others into disciples of Christ.

True discipleship is where you reproduce yourself in the life of someone else. That's what Jesus did with his disciples. The person whom you are discipling will understand Christlikeness by what they see in you.

> *"... everyone who is fully trained will be like his teacher." (discipler)*
> **Luke 6:40**

That's what discipleship is all about. Its about reproducing yourself in the .life of someone else **so that they in turn can reproduce THEIR life in someone else ... who in turn ...**

Paul instructs Timothy in a strategy of making disciples:

> *And the things you have heard me say in the presence of many witnesses entrust to reliable men who will also be qualified to teach others.*
> **2 Timothy 2:2**

5. The 3-step strategy to making disciples

It was with that understanding that we moved forward to revolutionise the way we "made disciples" at Crossfire. Instead of having bible studies about discipleship, we actually went and made disciples. Instead of just having programmes for "evangelism" ... and then "bible study" ... and then "leadership training" .. we intentionally set out to follow Jesus' model and actually made disciples. We aimed to bring people to Christ; to build them up in Christ, and to send them out for Christ.

By following the example of Jesus, by following the command of Jesus, we sought to implement a biblical strategy that would effectively "make disciples of all nations".

Here is the third and final "question and answer" that we expect all adults and students on our ministry team to memorise and actualise. This 3 step strategy is reflected in Figure 9.2

"How do we make disciples?"

**"By bringing our friends to Christ;
by building each other up in Christ;
and by sending us out for Christ.**

Figure 9.2

3. Sending Out

2. Building up

1. Bringing In

It is this 3 step strategy which controls and governs everything else we do. It is this 3 step strategy that decides what our programme will look like. It is this 3 step strategy which is explained in detail in the next chapters of this book.

6. How do you know that you're really 'making disciples'?

In one sense you can never sit back and confidently say "I have made a disciple". Discipleship is always about growing. It is always about going further. Discipleship is an ongoing passion in anyone's life. It needs to be ongoing in our lives – and it certainly needs to be ongoing in the lives of our students. Making disciples is also a team effort. You might be the principal "discipler" of another person, but there are other Christians who need to be involved in the process.

The mark of a true disciple is not that they are attending – or even that they are professing faith in Jesus ... or planted in a small group ... or being trained as a leader. The mark of someone who is a trained disciple is that they are able to go and help make a disciple of someone else. They know how to bring someone to Christ; they know to build someone up in Christ they know how to send them out for Christ.

Making a disciple is not the result of a series of programmes. It is not simply the communicating of information. I know of one youth ministry which runs its "discipleship" programme as a video series which individual students borrow, and complete the appropriate assignments. That might be a great way of getting important information across to a disciple, but it will not "make a disciple". Following Jesus' model, disciple-making is always **relational** where the life of one maturing disciple is reproduced in someone else.

So how do we know when we are "making a disciple" of one of our students?

Here are some of the basic questions we will ask:

a) **Have they truly come to Christ?** Is there a decision to follow Jesus which is evident in their day to day life? Are they showing true faith and ongoing repentance?

b) **Are they truly growing in Christ?** Are they planted in a small group where God's word is being sown into their life? Are they growing the heart of a disciple from John 15? (see Chapter 5 of this book). Are they being held accountable for their growth, their life and their ministry?

c) **Are they ministering to others?** Are they being filled with a passion to reach a world which is lost? Are they praying for their unsaved friends and seeking to win them for Christ?

And I believe this is the crunch question:

d) **Are they starting to be able to help reproduce the previous 3 steps in the life of someone else?**

That's what "making disciples" is all about. That is the big vision that God has in mind for your youth ministry. There is a world that is crying out to be brought to Christ. Whether you are ministering to 5 students or 500 students, God wants you to "make disciples of all nations".

He wants you to start by "making disciples" of those students that he has brought into your care. He wants you to be a faithful shepherd in raising them up as world-changers. He wants you to raise up strong disciples and effective disciple-makers who will make a mark for him long after they have left the realm of your youth ministry. He wants you to grow "fruit that will last".

7. Where do you start?

If you realise that God is calling you to "shift focus" in your youth ministry – to become passionate about really "making disciples' – and producing "fruit that will last" – where do you start?

That was a question I had to consider many years ago. I had been challenged from God's Word that it was time for a change. Rather than just "running youth groups and bible studies", I was convicted that God was calling us to make disciples; that is, to bring students to Christ, to build them up in Christ; and then to send them out for him, so that they in turn could bring their friends to Christ, help build them up, and help send them out.

I knew things had to change. We had all the youth group structure in place – we did all the things that good youth ministries were meant to do, but we weren't making disciples. We weren't building fruit that would last.

The starting point had to be with my leaders. There is no use bringing in a brand new plan if you don't have your leadership team onside. So I called together my "Team Leaders". Every ministry group in Crossfire had a team of leaders, and there were two Team Leaders who were overall in charge of each team. We had 6 different ministries – this gave me a team of 12 Team Leaders. Up until that time I had had a sort of "administrative" relationship with them, but I knew I had to start a "discipling relationship" with them. If my ultimate aim was to make disciples of our high school students, then I had to start by making disciples of my leaders.

I called them together. I shared my heart with them. I laid before them a vision of impacting our world by making disciples of our high schoolers. I challenged them about their own discipleship, and let them know where we were going to head in the coming year. Here was the deal; if they were going to be a Team Leader in the coming year, they were going to be discipled by me. I wanted them to pull out of whatever Young Adult Bible Study they were already in, and join a small group that I would be running for them. We were going to meet each week around God's Word; I would train them as disciples; I would spend personal time with them and hold them accountable for their growth; and I wanted then to hold me accountable as well.

This resulted in a variety of reactions. There were a few who enthusiastically said "This is what I've been waiting for, for years!" Others accepted the decision happily enough, but weren't really sure why we were doing it. A third group fought against it – I think one dropped out, and another one or two came along the next year a little reluctantly, but it was the beginning of a brand new relationship between my Team Leaders and me.

I had no idea of what to do. No-one had ever discipled me! Maybe you are in the same situation! If no-one has ever discipled you, I want to assure you that you can start the ball rolling so that a whole generation of discipled students will begin to impact this world for Christ. I was looking around for somewhere to start. I commenced by teaching through the topics in the appendix in Leroy Eim's book *"The Lost Art of Disciple Making"*. I'm sure I got lots of things wrong. I know I was an ineffective discipler in many ways. But God used my passion, and built my relationship with my Team Leaders, so that now, many years later, I can see a whole generation of students who have been discipled because of those leaders.

Discipling my key leaders was the most fruitful thing I had ever done in youth ministry. A whole new relationship developed over the years, and hundreds of teenagers have benefited as a result. I have to admit – we lost some leaders when we made the change to be a disciple-making youth ministry. They genuinely thought that we would turn all the kids off. But God was leading us on a bold adventure.

Start with your leaders. Train them as disciples. Fill them with a passion for making disciples of all nations. And then unleash them on your students.

Be prepared to be patient. Jesus spent 3 years with his men. Have you got this longer term vision for your work? Will you stay in youth ministry long enough to see the fruit of your labour? Will you produce fruit that will last?

How to Grow A Strategy That Will Last

SECTION 4

Chapter 10
The Strategy of "Bringing In"

Four Strategy Principles for "Bringing In"

1. Evangelism Must Be Top Priority

a) 2 Traps For Youth Groups

"Bringing In" describes the first step a person takes in being trained as a faithful disciple and effective disciple-maker. It's where a person is brought to Christ. It's where he is "converted". It's where he is changed from being God's enemy into becoming God's friend. It's where he is "saved". This is the process of helping a student to become a Christian. No further meaningful growth can happen until this vital first step is taken. Without this step there is no eternity with God, no forgiveness of sin, no eternal life, no …

So it should be simple. Every individual Christian in the world would keep personal evangelism as their top priority. Right? And every Christian youth ministry in the world would be passionately excited to keep evangelism as their top priority.

True?

Sadly, it is far from true. Many youth ministries which **start out** as being evangelistic, just settle back into being comfortable. They've got their kids – they've become a cosy group, and they just have nice bible studies which the Christian students all love. There is warm feedback - everyone feels included – everyone gets what they want.

But no new disciples are made. And the devil feels very comfortable.

As I look at dozens of youth ministries over many years, there appears to be 2 main traps that they fall into:

i Some have no biblical purpose or direction, and merely run time-occupying activities. (That is, they haven't worked out their biblical purpose or mission – and they should go back and re-read the last 2 chapters!)

ii Those that **do** have a biblical purpose and mission can often slip back to having nearly all their ministries aimed at the already-convinced Christians.

b) The "Balance" Test

Think about your own youth programme. In the average month, how many activities do you have that are primarily aimed at "building up" Christians, and how many activities do you have that are primarily aimed at "bringing in" students to become Christians?

A simple question. Is it well balanced?

For many dedicated, biblical youth ministries, the trap can work like this:

- Every month you have 4 weekly church services, which are mainly aimed at the Christians
- Every month you have 4 weekly youth groups, which are mainly aimed at Christians
- Every month you have 4 weekly Sunday School classes, which are mainly aimed at Christians
- Every month you have 4 weekly small bible study groups, which are mainly aimed at Christians
- Every month you have one "outreach" event

Monthly total: **"Building Up" (growth) Events** **= 16**
"Bringing In" (evangelism) Events **= 1**

Ouch! A 16 to 1 ratio! Now I know your youth ministry programme would never be as out-of-balance as this one, but do the exercise anyway, and see how you stack up.

I have seen surveys which suggest that about 80% of all Christian youth group activities are usually aimed at the "insider" – the already converted. And whilst many of these are **good biblical activities**, it is the **balance** which is the problem. By pouring so many resources into "building up" activities, evangelism is neglected; the "not-yet-saved" are neglected; and no new growth comes into the group, It might feel great to everyone who comes, but these are sure signs of a youth ministry which is starting to die.

c) 3 Results from "Out Of Balance" Youth Ministries

The effects of this problem are devastating!

i   Your Existing Christian Students Will Not Grow Healthy

Whilst the Christian student who is already in the system has an easy ride with cosy ministries, they do not grow to become strong disciples or effective disciple makers. You can't just feed students the bible and expect they will become spiritually fit! Good food alone does not produce fitness! If you just ate lots of good quality nutritious food, it might be fun, but it would not make you fit – it would make you fat! If you just feed Christian students lots of good quality bible teaching – they might well enjoy it, but it will not make them spiritually fit; it will make them spiritually fat!

As well as good food, they need good exercise. Their "exercise" is the ministry they will have. The most crucial part of this ministry will be to help win their friends for Christ. We'll look at this more in Chapter 12, but the first result of a lack of evangelism in your programme will be that your existing Christian students will not grow strongly.

ii   You Will Not Make Any New Disciples

If almost everything you do is aimed at the "already convinced", then you will lose touch with the dying world which needs the saving grace of Jesus. You will not see new students become

Christians. You will not reach the very people whom God has placed for you to reach. Your youth group will get more and more inward looking, and lose touch with the outside world completely. And as your group gets older and leaves, your ministry will eventually die out.

iii The Devil Will Be Happy

You can have as many bible studies as you like – but as long as your Christian students are not making any impact on the world, the devil is quite satisfied. One of his best strategies is simply to keep Christians busy, so they do not have time to advance God's kingdom. Bible study is a great activity – but if it's all you do, the devil can relax, because you will never impact this world and upset his plans.

d) 2 Reasons Behind The Problem

If the problem is so huge – and the results are so devastating – why does it occur? How is it that good and Godly youth ministries which have a passion to serve Jesus, can back off from this most crucial of ministries – evangelism?

i Everyone Loves "Fellowship"

Christian Students love it when you focus all your attention on them. If they really want to grow as Christians they'll be enthralled when you teach them the bible in a creative and relevant way. They will be loved and cared for in a cosy and accepting environment. Christian Parents love it because they want somewhere "nice" for their teenager to hang out, and a caring Christian environment is exactly what they want. Your leaders will love it too, because it means they will be deeply appreciated by co-operative students, and not torn down by the more demanding pagan hordes.

ii It Feels So Good

When you have a programme that almost exclusively targets the already-convinced Christians, it can create such a great atmosphere. It could be a little taste of heaven. Every Christian community should create an atmosphere of love, because we are all centred on the God of love. I love having Christians together as **part** of what we do; but if it is the **sum total** of what you do, you will miss out big time.

Let's get back to the priority of evangelism. It is not "Number 1" because it is more important than any other Christian ministry, but simply because – if we don't put it first, then we will never do it! The lure of "discipleship", "worship" "fellowship" or "unity" (all great things!) will tempt us away from the hard work of evangelism. Let's make it top priority to ensure that evangelism is central to everything we do.

2. Evangelism Is NOT Necessarily The First Step!

a) You Need To Grow Your Ministry Team First

So – now you might be thinking –"We've got to get out there and evangelise! We've got to change all our programmes so the central thrust of our youth ministry is evangelism. More outreach nights; more street ministry . Come on ... let's go!"

Whoa! Just hang on! Even though evangelism should be our top priority – it doesn't mean that it's necessarily the starting point! The only situation I can imagine where evangelism would be your starting point in youth ministry is if you are the **only Christian** in youth ministry in your church! You are then in "desert island" ministry where everything is up to you! (And even then, your starting point should be prayer!)

But if you have at least one other Christian in youth ministry with you – whether that be an adult or a student, then your starting point is not to go out and evangelise – it is to "build up" the other Christians, sow into them a passion for evangelism, and then involve them in an intentional evangelism ministry with you. Otherwise you will just go off on a "one person Rambo-mission" to save the planet ... but you will never develop a structure that multiplies your ministry – you will never develop the leaders and fellow workers that God has placed with you - you will never establish a ministry that will thrive and prosper long after you have left it - and you will never develop "fruit that will last"

Look at the ministry of Jesus. His heart was to "seek and save what was lost" (Luke 19:10) But he started his public ministry by gathering his ministry team, and discipling them.

b) You Might Be Overwhelmed With Non-Christians!

If you go chasing non-Christian students in a frenzy of evangelistic fervour – without first building up your existing Christians and equipping your ministry team, whilst this might be an very exciting time for you, you may find a number of difficulties which might tend to overwhelm you.

   i Your leaders might burn out quickly

If you race into evangelism, with inadequate leadership resources, your existing leaders will easily get burnt out. They might have a deep love for the non-Christian students who come, but if your leaders are too few in number- or if they are poorly trained (or not trained at all!), they will be quickly exhausted, and give up.

   ii You might get behavioural difficulties.

If you have very few Christian Students, and large numbers of non-Christian students, then the non-Christian students will set the "norm" for behaviour in your group. They will bring to the group whatever values are instilled in their lives, and if they are the dominant group, you may well find that you spend so much time on discipline, that your real ministry never gets through.

   iii You Will Not Reach Those Who Want To Respond.

If you are over-run with non-Christian students, you may find real difficulty in ministering to those who are indeed responding. If the "non-responsive" group dominates, it makes it exceedingly difficult for those who want to respond to Jesus to do so publicly. And even if they do, your time will be so occupied in "controlling the masses" that you might not be able to spend time with the very ones who need you most.

iv You Will Not Produce "Fruit That Will Last"

You produce "fruit that will last" by personally sowing into the lives of others, and gradually multiplying your ministry. Going for the vast masses "in one hit" may bring some into God's kingdom – but you are not set up to disciple them and you will risk them withering on the vine. And will **you** last? Can you take the constant drain of frustrating ministry? If you leave, will the ministry survive at all?

I made this mistake at a church once. We had a "steady as it goes" older youth ministry (young adults). We had about half a dozen high schoolers who attended a Sunday Morning programme. I had established a Scripture Ministry at the local State High School and was developing good relationships with non-Christian students. Many were asking questions. I wanted an evangelistic group I could invite them to. I wanted to see them won to Christ's kingdom and implanted in his church.

I grabbed our young adult group and asked "Who will lead?" A handful of enthusiastic helpers responded. I grabbed our 6 Christian high-schoolers. "Would you come? Would you bring your friends?" They said they'd check it out. I stood up at the local high school assembly and announced our new youth group and invited one and all to show up.

30 pagan kids showed up the first night. Our 6 Christian kids were never to be seen after this point! 40 pagans came on the second night. 50 on the third. It was wild! It was chaotic! It was out of control! The behaviour was uncontrollable. We could not enforce a reasonable standard of discipline. Leaders were attacked with rocks. Fights developed. The police had to be called.

I should say that in the middle of this chaos, one or two students decided to follow Jesus. But the cost was too high. Many leaders were "burned". The "nice" kids stayed away – it was too wild for them. We wanted to befriend these kids – instead we became their disciplinarians.

I learnt a strong lesson from this. **Don't start solo with evangelism!** Build your ministry team and disciple your Christian students first. As you sow into them a passion and a heart to see their friends saved, they will come to you and say "Can we start a group to bring our unsaved friends to where they can hear the gospel?" **Then** you know that they are ready to work in partnership with you. Then you know that you are ready to build "fruit that will last".

3. Your Students Are Your Best Evangelists

a) The Danger of "Pastor-Centred" Evangelism

When I started in youth ministry, I had big dreams for what could be done, When it came to evangelism, all those dreams and plans centred around me. I mean, I was the full-time Youth Pastor, wasn't I? I was the one who had trained at Theological College. I was the one with the lifelong passion to see high-schoolers grow as disciples of Christ. I had been trained in how to share the gospel effectively. I had big dreams and plans for evangelism. And God, being the gracious God that he is, allowed some of these plans to prosper.

I was able to have a ministry at the local high school. I had the privilege of helping some students to come to Christ, right there in the schoolyard! Many students would come and talk with me personally. Many times I had the opportunity to share the gospel with them and bring them to Christ. At our youth group - at church - at camps – I was enabled to proclaim the gospel through preaching – and when I asked for students to respond, many came forward and submitted their lives to Jesus. I was as happy as a koala bear in a gum tree! I loved sharing the gospel. I loved bringing students to Christ! And I was getting paid for it!

This can be one of the greatest traps in youth ministry. Yes, God works through all this foolishness, but if I am the main one who keeps bringing students to Christ, then we will only ever **add** to God's kingdom. But I believe he has called upon us to not just add but to **multiply** the ministry of his kingdom by equipping others to be passionate disciples and effective disciple makers.

If I am the one who brings every kid to Christ, what happens when I am no longer around? If I am the one who is always asking people to respond to the gospel, how can we say that we're equipping our students to be "fishers of men"? If every ministry flows through me, am I really growing "fruit that will last"?

b) Every Student Has A Ministry

There is no way that Crossfire would have an effective ministry if it wasn't for the active ministry of our students. It would just be a programme which some students might happen to turn up to. Don't misunderstand me. I am not saying that every one of our students is a skilled evangelist. Probably very few of them are. (We are working on that!)

But we are aiming to fill every one of our Christian students with a passion to reach their unsaved friends. We want every student to be praying for their unsaved friends. We want every student to be inviting their friends to Crossfire and other evangelistic opportunities. (This is our PEER Ministry Programme – see later chapters). Our ministry depends on our students being faithful in their ministry.

This is dangerous stuff – but this is also exciting stuff. Christian students will reach other students that we could never reach. They have networks of friendship that go far beyond what us "oldies" can achieve. They have a credibility when they share the gospel because they're not "the professionals".

You see, our mission is not to "bring students to Christ". Our mission is "to make disciples of all nations". We can never reach out around this planet until we **multiply** our ministry by equipping our students to reach out to their friends.

I would never want to start up an intentional evangelistic ministry until I had first put the time in to make disciples of our Christian students. Disciple the christians first – and equip them to be a ministry team who will have a passion to reach out in partnership with you to see their friends saved.

More about this later!

4. God's Gospel Works!

"I am not ashamed of the gospel, because it is the power of God for the salvation of everyone who believes"
Romans 1:16

Do you believe that? Do you really believe that the gospel is the power of God to save those who believe?

"Of course I do!" you vehemently declare! "What do you think I am?"

I can remember when I was challenged on that same question. "Do you believe that the gospel is the power of God to save those who believe?"

"Why do you ask that?"
"Because your programme shows that you don't believe it"
"What do you mean?"

My questioner was one of those annoying youth pastors who asks hard questions about difficult subjects. He pointed out to me some things which I was probably deliberately avoiding. It had to do with where we were putting our effort.

"You think that it's your **packaging** of the gospel that has the power to save those who believe! You think that if you just present the gospel the right way – if you have the most conducive atmosphere - if you have the loudest music - if you carefully plan some really fun activities – if you bring the smoke machine in at just the right time – if you can tell right story … you believe that it's the **way** you present things that really matters. Cos that's where you're putting all your time and effort. Why don't you just trust that the gospel will work?"

I was stunned. How could I have missed the mark so widely?

When we made big changes to Crossfire, we wanted to show that we absolutely trusted God's gospel. Yes – we still wanted to make our ministry as creative and relevant as possible. But we weren't going to disguise the gospel by preaching sermons about "Peer Pressure – Part 6" – we weren't going to tack a little "devotional" on the end of a games night; we weren't going to engineer the atmosphere to try and get students to respond. We were going to openly proclaim Jesus from the Scriptures – and centre our message on his death and resurrection,

The result? Fruit that lasts. God's gospel really works! Try it! Stop hiding your message by tacking a 5 minute devotional on the end of a "Crazy Music" night. Stop skating around the message of Jesus by having endless nights on "Coping with my braces", "Dealing with my pimples". Exciting as these are, **they do not have the power to save those who believe!**

I was being interviewed for a youth pastor's position at a church many years ago. I was talking with the then outgoing youth pastor to get an idea of where the ministry was centred, he described for me a monthly outreach night that they were running – where they intentionally wanted to reach new students and start involving them in following Jesus.

Here is the promise they made to their Christian students. "You can have complete confidence in bringing your non-Christian friends to our outreach night. You will not be embarrassed at all. We guarantee it will be a great night, and we guarantee that we will not mention the gospel"

I was stunned, An outreach night where they guaranteed they would not mention the gospel? My goodness! Has the world suddenly gone crazy? How on earth can you bring people to Christ if you don't mention the gospel? Aarrgghh!!

At Crossfire, we make 2 guarantees to our Christian students to give them confidence to invite their unsaved friends along.

i. Every night we will proclaim Jesus from the Scriptures. It is always the right night to bring an unsaved friend because we will always proclaim the gospel.

ii We won't be complete idiots in the way we do it.

"I am not ashamed of the gospel, because it is the power of God for the salvation of everyone who believes"
Romans 1:16

Do you believe it? Are you game to tell your keyboard player not to play tinkling little notes as you ask students to come forward for Jesus? Or do you believe the keyboard has the power to save those who believe? Are you prepared to base your whole message on what the bible says rather than trotting out that cutting emotional story you learnt in youth leaders' school? Will your programme- and your advertising really reflect that you trust the gospel to save all who believe?

Where do you and your leaders put their time and effort in preparing for your weekly youth group?

Is it in the proclamation of the gospel – or is it in your packaging?

The gospel **is** the power of God to save those who believe. It really works! And it is the only thing that will build "fruit that will last"

Now ... to build and grow that fruit ...

Chapter 11
The Strategy of "Building Up"

Four Strategy Principles for "Building Up"

1. Build with the end result in mind

"Building Up" is not an end in itself.

Go to any decent church, and you will see they are great believers in this "building up" ministry. Most churches have a whole network of small groups to cater for all sorts of needs across a wide range of ages. We all know they're great. We all know that we really need them.

But go up to any small bible study group and ask them this question "Why are you meeting?", and you'll get some interesting answers.

"Why are you meeting in a small group each week?"
   "To study the bible"
"And why do you want to study the bible?"
   "So we get to know God better"
"Why is it important to get to know God better?"
   "So we will grow stronger as Christians"
"Why do you want to grow stronger as Christians?"
   "So we ... um ... er ..."

All these reasons are great things. I am all in favour of people studying the bible, getting to know God better, becoming stronger as Christians ... but we've still got to answer the question "**Why** are these things so important? Why are we really meeting week by week in a small bible study group?"

We gather together around God's word for the same reason that Jesus gathered his disciples around him. *"... that they might be with him and that he might send them out ..." (Mark 3:14).* We gather together to be built up **so that we might be effective as we are sent out!** The true test of whether a bible study group is going well is not "are we learning a lot" or "do we have warm fellowship together" (important as these things are!) Here is the important question to answer: As a result of us meeting together "in here" – are we more effective for Christ "out there"? If the answer is "yes", the small group is worth doing; if the answer is "no", then the small group is wasting everyone's time.

I love being looked after. I love being waited on hand and foot. It is superb when other Christians overwhelm me with love. Caring, loving fellowship is one of the amazing by-products of belonging to God's people. I want to be part of a genuinely loving body of believers where we support and uphold each other with acts of random kindness.

But the beauty of "fellowship" creates the biggest trap or us. We can learn to love it so much that we lose focus on **why** God has called us to himself and left us on the planet. You will discover in churches and youth ministries Christians who just want to be "looked after". They will complain if too much emphasis is placed on evangelism. "This is **my** church! Why should we change the way we've done things for the sake of the outsiders?" But that is precisely the nature of being God's pilgrim people here on planet earth. We **will** do anything for the sake of the outsiders.

We build Christians up so that **they** can be sent out for Christ!

2. Build with the Right Tools

What tools do you think will "build up" the young disciples that God has placed into your care? Here are 3 clues from the Scriptures as to what to sow into your young disciples:

a) The Grace of God's Word

> *"Now I commit you to God and to the word of his grace, which can*

build you up and give you an inheritance among all those who are sanctified".
Acts 20:32

God's Word is the substance that "building up" is made of. Everything we need to know to live the life that God wants for us is contained in his word. Students are not built up on hype, or on endless activities, or ever increasing decibels of contemporary music (fun though they might be). If you are serious about growing, you will sow God's word into them at every opportunity.

b) The Power of God's Love

"Knowledge puffs up, but love builds up".
1 Corinthians 8:1

"Each of us should please his neighbour for his good, to build him up".
Romans 15:2

When God's love is displayed through God's people, amazing results will be seen. There is nothing that builds up like a positive experience of genuine love. This is something that we try to model consistently. As the youth pastor, I need to set an example of love in the way I deal with leaders and students - both the co-operative and the unco-operative. I need to model a community of love in my own family life, and in my relationships with my key leaders. At every opportunity I need to encourage genuine love when the Christian community meets – and when they are scattered to their separate houses.

c) The Ministry of God's People

It's when the whole body of Christ is working together – caring for each other – serving each other – when every believer gives of themselves for the sake of the whole body – the whole body grows. Every believer is built up!

"From him the whole body, joined and held together by every supporting ligament, grows and builds itself up in love, as each part does its work".
Ephesians 4:16

When you are sowing into many others – and encouraging them to use whatever gift God has given them to serve others – especially when those gifts are the ones that plant God's word into someone else's life – then you will build up every believer in the church.

> *"So it is with you. Since you are eager to have spiritual gifts, try to excel in gifts that build up the church".*
> **1 Corinthians 14:12**

The effect that one individual can have on another cannot be over-estimated. When you pour your life into another believer – and actively encourage them – then everything you do with them – everything you say to them will build them up.

The ministry of encouragement can unleash unparalleled growth in another believer

> *"Therefore encourage one another and build each other up, just as in fact you are doing".*
> **1 Thessalonians 5:11**

3. Build with Accountability

God can build people up in an amazing number of ways. His word is powerful and will have a profound effect on the genuine disciple. Many of us could remember being present at a church service where a powerful sermon has had a dramatic effect on our walk as a Christian.

But to intentionally build up a disciple, you need more than powerful sermons. You need to develop accountability. That is, that as members of the one body, we are not just answerable to God for our lives, but we are answerable to each other. There is no such thing as a "private sin which doesn't affect anyone else". Everything I do affects the other Christians around me. In our discipling, I want to build up this accountability so that we can support each other in times of need.

> *"Therefore confess your sins to each other and pray for each other so that you may be healed."*
> **James 5:16**

By confessing our sins to each other, we are helping to hold each other accountable so that the whole body will be "built up."

Andrew* is one of the young men in our youth leadership team and he came to me one day to talk about his relationship with his girlfriend. There were many good aspects to this relationship, but physically they were growing too close too fast and they were in borderline areas as far as obedience and purity was concerned. They were keen to deal with the difficulties in their relationship, so that they might model Christlikeness in everything they did.

It seemed right for the relationship to continue, but the temptation was strong. How did we deal with it? Very simply, he has made himself accountable to me. It is okay for me to ask him specific questions about how things are going in this relationship. He knows I will ask hard questions. He knows that one of my questions will be "Andrew, are you hiding anything from me?" It's not an interrogation. It's not a confessional. It is simply one Christian making himself accountable to another Christian so that the whole body is built up.

"Therefore confess your sins to each other and pray for each other so that you may be healed."
James 5:16

I coach a Discipleship Team ("D-Team"). I have a small team of high school boys who are striving to grow as followers of Jesus. You will learn more about our D-Teams in Chapter 14. But one of the keys to "building up" disciples in these small groups is "accountability". That is, we are answerable to each other because we are all members of the same body. Not answerable to each other so we can tear each other down; but answerable to each other to build each other up.

This "accountability" comes down to the standards we have for our group. Let me tell you something I noticed about small groups around the Christian world. **Often the local soccer coach has higher standard for his team than a bible study leader has for his group!** Here is what

I mean. Imagine you are a member of a local soccer team. Every week you have a training night. Every week you play a game. What would happen if you just didn't bother to show up at training? What would happen if you only came to matches "when you felt like it?" Any decent coach would not tolerate this for long, and you might find that your no longer have a place on the team! I coach a junior soccer team, and if anyone cannot make it to training, they must notify me first. If I don't hear from them – I will call them myself to chase them up. I expect everyone to show up at every game – unless they have notified me. It is not acceptable to simply "miss a game" and let the team down.

While I don't want our D-teams to major in "kicking kids out", I still expect them to have at least as high a standard as a local soccer coach. We are accountable to each other. I never want to look around my D-Team and simply not know why students are missing. If I have asked people to memorise a verse from the bible, I expect them to have it done. While we can be understanding, forgiving, and accepting of difficult circumstances that some students are in, it will pay dividends to keep the standard high.

The same is true in the way we teach the bible. Learning from God's word is a major focus of our D-teams. But we don't teach God's word so that students will know God's word. We teach God's word so that our students will **live** God's word

> *"Do not merely listen to the word, and so deceive yourselves. Do what it says."*
> ***James 1:22***

A soccer coach is the same. A soccer coach doesn't teach his team about soccer so they will know lots of information about soccer. He teaches them about soccer so they will **play** soccer well. He tells them; he shows them; he does it with them; he corrects; he stands with them while they do it; he then lets them adopt their own style while he cheers from the sidelines.

To really "build up" disciples, you must hold them accountable for putting into practice what they are learning. If I am teaching my group from the Scriptures about the importance of spending regular individual time with

God – I don't just teach them the information, and leave it there. I will help them make a plan for how they will spend individual time with God on a regular basis. Then on the following week, we will all check through our plans to see how we went. I am as accountable as the rest of the group. I expect them to ask me how things are. We hold each other up and build each other up this way.

So what happens when a student says "I didn't open my bible all week. I didn't get to spend any time with God at all"?

The "non-accountable" leader will reply "That's okay, we all have hard weeks. Don't worry about it". The "over-accountable" leader will reply "That's just not good enough. You're letting the team down. Don't do it again"

But I want to develop a culture of accountability that has genuine Christlike concern for each person. I hope our D-team coaches would respond to that situation by saying "Wow – that must have been a hard week for you. Tell us a bit about it". Once they have worked through what the problems were, a D-team coach should then say "How can we deal with the upcoming week so you don't get into the same problem again? How can I help you with this?" You can still have accountability and Christlike love at the same time! And without love - and without accountability – you will not truly "build up" disciples.

Check out the methods that you have in place to "build up" your Christian students. And then check up whether you have built in "accountability". Without it, you might fall into the trap of raising up Christians to be "hearers" rather than "doers."

4. Build with the Right Trainers

One key thing I have learned over the past 21 years about "building up" young Christians is this: **The person who is the "trainer" is far more important than the teaching materials that are being used.** Essentially, making disciples is not a course, nor a curriculum. It is the implanting of the passion to follow Jesus from one person to another. It's the learning of Christlikeness by seeing it in operation in an older and wiser Christian. It's reproducing in someone else the enthusiasm and ability to not only be faithful as a disciple, but effective as a disciple maker.

Sermons have a vital place in building up Christians. So does the music of praise and worship. Good books and videos can be a vital supplement. But the essence of "building up" disciples is that you sow God's word into them in the context of a personal relationship. We don't do "one on one" discipling with high-schoolers (there are good legal reasons to avoid this), but we do focus very much on small groups, where one adult Christian is able to sow into the lives of half a dozen high-school Christians.

Sure – we use a curriculum – and I have authored several books to help this "building up" to occur ("Growing Young Disciples" Series for Junior High; "Discipleship Training" for Senior High). But the key to developing strong and faithful disciples is to ensure that the person building them up is walking faithfully with Jesus every step of the way. I would rather have the right person teaching a "second best" bible-curriculum, than a second best trainer teaching "first rate" material. I want to have confidence in the life and ministry of the adult leader; then I will know at what standard he will build up those in his care.

I believe that the most important thing that any of our youth leaders at St. Paul's will do is to disciple some young people. Everything they do should point to this part of their ministry. The greatest amount of time, effort, concern and care should go to the individuals that make up their D-Team.

The small number of young people that they invest their life into will become the godly men and women, the mums and dads, the missionaries, pastors and leaders of our community and world. The future of the church in general depends on how faithfully we carry out the command of 2 Timothy 2:2 *"And the things you have heard me say in the presence of many witnesses entrust to reliable men who will also be qualified to teach others"*

Our D-Team Coaches enter a very privileged relationship with some valued people in God's kingdom. They disciple a small group of Christian high schoolers. Their relationship will be special and unique.

Because this is a privileged relationship, leaders need to be careful of a number of things:

- that their relationship will always point those in their care towards Christ.
- that they will continue in the relationship for the benefit of the other person - not for what they are getting out of it themselves.
- that they will always have the goal of making the student independent of them as they grow more dependent on God.

Our aim for our students is that as they grow as disciples they will grow **less dependent** on their discipleship trainer, and **more dependent** on God. This is a fine balance, but it is key to successful discipling.

God wants you to build up these disciples – so that He can send them out!

Chapter 12
The Strategy of "Sending Out"

Four Strategy Principles for "Sending Out"

1. Start At The Very Beginning

It's interesting to watch Jesus as he commences his public ministry. He moves forward, calling people to follow him, so that ...

So that what? When Jesus calls people to follow him, what is it that he enlists them for? You can imagine the scene. Jesus is in his very early days of ministry. People are starting to hear about him. Some have heard his teaching. There is an air of anticipation.

He walks beside the Sea of Galilee, and he sees two brothers – Simon and Andrew. There they are, casting their nets into the lake as they continue their life of fishing. Jesus walks over to them and says "Come follow me, and "...

STOP!

If you were Jesus, how would you have finished that sentence? Come on – get rid of any memory verses that are springing to your mind ... honestly now - how would you have finished that sentence?

"Come follow me ... and I will give you eternal life"?
"Come follow me ... and I will make you my friends"?
"Come follow me ... and I will give you lasting satisfaction that fishing will never bring"?
"Come follow me ... and I will enliven you with some impactful preaching"?

"Come follow me ... and I will put you in a cosy small group for some warm fellowship"

What would you have said?

Honestly?

> "Come, follow me," Jesus said, "and I will make you fishers of men."
> **Matthew 4:19**.

Fishers of men.

Jesus says to these first disciples "If you follow me, I will give you a ministry to others."

Jesus says "Follow me, because I want you as part of my ministry team."

Jesus says "Come and be built up with me – so that I may send you out for me."

As we have noted earlier:

> "He appointed twelve—designating them apostles— that they might be with him and that he might send them out to preach ..."
> **Mark 3:14**

No ten-week training course. No bible college diploma. No accreditation from a major denomination. Jesus just calls people to follow him, and he immediately enrols them on his ministry team.

This is not a call to take **anybody** – no matter how inappropriate – and place them on your leadership team. But it is a call to be biblical in our thinking that all believers are expected to have a ministry. They might never get a staff position in a church, but Jesus' expectation on every disciple is that they too will be an active disciple-maker.

I want all students who come to Christ through our ministry to know from Day 1 that Jesus wants them on his ministry team. They might not know what to do or how to do it; but from their first moments I want them to have a passion to reach their friends, and reach their world.

> **Brad*** and **Norman*** were two Year 10 students at the local High School. Through my contact at the school, I had developed a good

relationship with them, and had the opportunity to share the good news of Jesus with them. They were both responding positively, so we arranged to do a 5 week "Discovering Jesus" course at school – 5 lunchtimes over 5 weeks. During this time, both Brad and Norman made a commitment to follow Jesus.

The week after they made a commitment to follow Jesus, I caught up with them at school to plan the next step. "You've got a whole lifetime of learning to follow Jesus ahead of you. We're going to help you every step of the way. Now the first thing I want you to know is that Jesus wants you to help your friends discover the things that you've just discovered"

"You mean he wants us to help our friends become Christians?" asked Brad

"Exactly!"

Brad and Norman looked at each other and smiled. They turned to me and said "We'll be back." And they disappeared into the schoolyard. A few moments later they returned with two friends in tow. "This is Sam and Allen. They want to do 'Discovering Jesus' too!"

I chatted with their friends. They seemed genuine. So we started **another** "Discovering Jesus" Course – with Brad and Norman sitting in and helping their friends to discover Jesus for the first time.

New Christians are absolutely the best at bringing new people along to things. New people bring new people. I want them to have a passion for their unsaved friends from the word "go". If they are new Christians, then they don't yet understand that the Christian Church is full of people who can't be bothered about having a ministry in this world. They will find this out later. But I want them to be passionate to minister to others right from the very beginning.

"Come, follow me," Jesus said, "and I will make you fishers of men."
Matthew 4:19.

You are shaping habits and priorities which will be part of these young disciples life for decades and decades. So start them off right - and prepare them for a lifetime of passionate and active ministry.

2. Focus On The Central Ministries

I know of many great youth ministries which quickly get their young people into ministry teams. Teenagers end up in Welcoming Teams, Drama Teams, Music Teams, Catering Teams, Dance Teams ... and all sorts of other good things for God's kingdom.

But as great as these things are, and as helpful as these ministries are, they can be a real distraction from the central ministry that Christ has called us to – to make disciples. Yes, I know that Welcoming Teams, Drama Teams, Music Teams etc are all helping to make disciples in their own way. And at our own church, we have high-schoolers in many of these ministries and they do an awesome job.

But I don't want them getting into these "specialist" ministries until they have first been involved in the central "every member" ministries – of Peer Care and Peer Witnessing.

That is, I don't want young 14 yr old Flossy to grow up thinking that her spiritual gift is "Dancing", and that her only way of helping to make disciples is to perform liturgical dance and interpret great Christian songs with body movement. Dance may well be one of her areas of gifting, **but I want her to know how to support and encourage her fellow Christians, and reach out to her non-Christian friends in her day to day life.**

I want her to be actively involved in the ministry of Peer Care and Peer Witnessing and to develop skills in these areas which will last her throughout her life. As she develops these central "every member" ministries, she will also enhance her dance ministry and integrate it much more into her overall passion to make disciples. If we're not careful, the "Welcoming teams, Music Teams" etc. might actually take our young people **away** from being passionately involved in disciple-making ministries.

It's interesting in the culture that I work in at the moment. Our church is situated in an upwardly mobile middle-class area of suburban Sydney. This is a great place to live, and I love being here! But because we are in a "upper" socio-economic community, and many parents invest heavily in their children's education, it seems like every second student at our church learns a musical instrument! I never cease to be amazed by the vast number of pianists, flautists, saxophonists, drummers etc. that we have in our youth ministry. If we wanted to , we could almost have every second student involved in a music ministry of some description! We could have musical groups and bands coming out of our armpits!

Why has God "blessed" us so abundantly? Why didn't this happen in my former church? Why were we struggling to find a young person who wanted to play music? We had hardly any. Why didn't God bless us that way in my former church?

There's no great theological reason here. It simply has to do with money. My former church was in a poorer community. There wasn't a lot of money around. No-one had money to buy musical instruments. No-one had money to pay for music lessons. It wasn't a value that was highly prized in the community.

I love the fact that we have so many talented young musicians at our church. But I would be mistaken if I thought I should steer them all into music ministry. **Some** of them may be used that way. But some of them only play an instrument because it was important for their parents to foster this in them!

I want every young disciple to understand the importance of encouraging and caring for their fellow Christians. This is an attitude that I want to last for the whole of their life. I want every young disciple to be centrally involved in actively reaching out to their non-Christian friends. I want them to be active disciple-makers for the rest of their life. I want them to be able to help make disciples whether they are on an official church ministry team or not.

That's the sort of ministry I mean, when I say "get your new Christian involved in ministry". (See details of our "PEER" Ministry Training in

Chapter 15). Once they have established their passion for Peer Care and Peer Witnessing (the "every member ministries"), then they are free to explore other areas of "Specialist" ministry.

3. Good Exercise Brings Healthy Passion

a) "Sending Out" produces healthy disciples

I wondered for many years why this crucial "Sending Out" step of "making disciples" so often got left out. Good churches with great evangelism programmes and solid youth ministries with effective bible teaching programmes often seem to stall at the "Sending Out" phase. They just sink back into being comfortable, cosy places where Christians get fat being fed on God's Word.

And then it hit me.

No-one likes to exercise! Sure – many of us are committed to exercise, and many of us enjoy the benefits of healthy exercise, and many of us have worked out enjoyable ways of doing regular exercise. ... but deep down ... not many of us want to do it! You watch a great TV show where you are motivated to start exercise - and you start a jogging programme - and it's great for 3 weeks ... but then you have a few late nights – a few rainy days – a couple of cold mornings - a few extra commitments, and it's not hard for your 3 weeks of jogging to be the only jogging you ever do! They tell me that the most "unused" piece of equipment in the average home is the exercise bike. A rush of enthusiasm ... some frantic cycling ... and then it all gets a bit hard and a little inconvenient, and the exercise bike is consigned to the back of the garage.

The same is true in the Christian Church. To be healthy we need good food. And God's Word is the best "food" you will get anywhere. But good food by itself will not make you fit! It will simply make you fat! It must be balanced with good exercise. Ministry is the "exercise" which will grow healthy Christians. We all know this. We all agree with this ...

But like exercise, ministry can be hard work. It is far more comfortable to have a bible study about "evangelism" than to actually get out and evangelise. It is easier to go to a conference on "Impacting the World" than to actually go out and impact the world. It is very rewarding to have a small bible study group where your focus is "fellowship", rather than a group that is equipping you for ministry "out there".

Disciple-making ministry will always take you out of your comfort zone. You will find yourself talking with people you might not normally talk with. You will find yourself being challenged in some very scary ways. Our natural inclination is to back away from these areas, and retreat to our comfort zone of warm fellowship and awesome worship. Certainly the devil has a vested interest in keeping us away from disciple-making ministries. If you have a vibrant youth ministry that has great bible study groups who have fantastic fellowship and huge mutual support – but this never turns into active ministry in the world that is dying – then the devil is probably very relaxed. He has nothing to fear.

All this might make it seem that ministry is just plain hard work. Well, in one sense it is. But once you involve your students in disciple-making ministries, you'll find there are some huge rewards.

b) "Sending Out" produces passionate disciples

"How do you keep your Christian students passionate in their faith?"

It's a question that I often get asked. I know what lies behind it.

There is usually no trouble in getting brand-new Christians to be passionate. They are pretty excited and enthusiastic about everything. But what about the "hardened" Christian student? You know, the teenager that comes from a Christian family, and attends a Christian Church and a Christian Youth Group. He is a pupil in a Christian school, and he plays on a Christian soccer team. He watches Christian TV and listens to Christian Music. He goes on Christian camps and plays in a Christian band. He lives in a lovely Christian house, where he plays with his Christian dog in his Christian garden …

Do you get the picture? Some students almost live in a Christian "prison". They never enter the real world, and for many of them, even though their personal faith in Jesus is genuine, they can be very apathetic, very critical, and stay right on the fringe of all your youth ministry. They believe in Jesus, but they never show any enthusiasm for following him.

How do you get these students to be passionate?

i Impart a big vision

Keep before them the big picture that God is raising them up to help impact this world for him. This is the big picture that Jesus left for us. Keep this big picture before them as their personal vision (See Chapter 9)

ii Involve them in a big ministry

The way to keep the troops passionate is to keep them in frontline ministry. In a war, the only soldiers who get complacent; the only troops who complain and whinge about their conditions; the only service personnel who lose their passion and enthusiasm are those who are relaxing back at the comfort of the base. The soldier in the front-line trench has no time for such negativism. His life is on the line. He is engaged in a life and death struggle and needs to be ever-alert for danger and opposition.

So too, when you put your students in front-line disciple-making ministries, they will keep their passion. When they are involved in active evangelism – even in Satan's turf – you will see a passion and enthusiasm which does not need to be artificially buoyed. That's why keeping an evangelistic focus is so vital to the health of your Christian disciples. That's why "sending them out" in front-line disciple-making ministries will keep their passion high as they serve their lord and witness first hand the victories he is winning.

Remember the "buzz" the first time you led someone to Christ? Give your students the same thrill as you equip them to impact this world for Christ.

4. Raise Up New Testament "Shepherds"

As we train and equip our student and adult ministry team, we need to keep before us the picture of what they are meant to be like. We want them to be "pastors" or "shepherds" the way the New Testament describes them. In the New International Version (NIV) the word "pastor" is only used once in the New Testament. But the word for "pastor" is the same word for "shepherd" and the New Testament has lots to say about what a shepherd is meant to be like.

Check how you are going in "Sending Out" your high school disciples and your adult leaders. Are you raising them up to be "New Testament Shepherds"?

a) The Three Relationships of a New Testament Shepherd

i   Know Christ, your shepherd

Jesus is the true shepherd. If you want to be a true shepherd, then immerse yourself in him, that you might show his love to others.

1 Peter 5: 2-4, Rev 7:17, 1 Peter 2:25

ii   Know Your Heart

Beware the ever present danger of being a false shepherd who looks after his own interests.

Matthew 7:15, Jude 1:12, 1 Peter 5:2-4

iii. Know Your Sheep

Just like Jesus, know each of your sheep personally.

John 10:2-4

b) The Three Tasks of a New Testament Shepherd

i   Find your Sheep

Never forget about the one who strays.

Matthew 12:11-12 Luke 15:4-7

ii Guard your sheep

Protect your sheep from wolves that will devour - even at the risk of your own life.

Acts 20:28-31, 1 Peter 2:25, Matthew 26:31, John 10: 7-18, John 10: 28-29

iii Feed your sheep

Guide them to the green pastures where they will feed on God's word and be equipped for active ministry.

John 21:15-17, Mark 6:34, Revelation 7:17, Ephesians 4:11-12

SECTION 5

How to Grow A Programme That Will Last

Chapter 13
Programming For "Bringing In"

"How To Grow A Programme That Will Last" is probably the wrong title for this section. What you really want is a programme that will produce RESULTS that will last. Your programme of course, is only a temporary means to achieve your unchanging biblical purposes. Your programme will change from year to year. The programme at your church may be very different from the programme at our church.

But let's have a look at programming. If we take all the biblical principles for disciple-making; if we develop a strategy of "Bringing In", "Building Up" and "Sending Out"; what might it look like in the youth ministry of a local church?

This is what it looks like in our church. Please do not think that our programme will fit your church automatically. But see if you can draw out the **principles** behind our programming – and apply it to your local situation in a way that will work for you.

1. The Joys and Dangers of Bridge-Building

"Bringing In" or "evangelistic" ministries are essentially "bridge building" exercises. We are attempting to establish a "bridge" between the people of God, and the people who do not yet belong to God. We want to form a conduit so that those who do not yet know Jesus might come to know him. We want a bridge that gets us Christians out into to the community, and a bridge that gets those people from the community to come into Christ.

What sort of a bridge should you build? One that will bring the traffic across! That is the essential nature of a bridge. That is why it exists.

It is there to bring traffic from Point A to Point B.

This is where evangelistic ministries can get into difficulty. Sometime we build a bridge that is so spectacular, that all we wan t to do is sit and admire the bridge after we've built it. The Christian Church is littered with great evangelistic ideas which turned into Gargantuan monuments!

> This is the trap our own Crossfire Groups fell into. Our Friday Night youth groups were a bridge into the community. We worked darn hard to make them an attractive bridge so that teenagers would want to come and use our bridge. Our groups were very attractive, and we put in heaps of effort to keep them that way. Our reputation as bridge builders was strong in the community, and many high-schoolers came to look at and enjoy our bridge.

> **But we weren't getting any traffic coming across!** Our bridge had become a monument, to admire, rather than a roadway to travel on. And we didn't have any strength left to try and get traffic to cross our bridge, because we were putting all our effort into making our bridges so darn attractive that everyone would come and look at them.

If you are running an evangelistic "bridge building" ministry at the moment, **check whether you are getting traffic to come across to God's kingdom!** Your programme is not the centrepiece of your ministry. Actual ministry is meant to be the centrepiece of your programme! If your outreach bridge is just a place where the Christians like to hang out admiring the view, or a place where non-Christians come for a look, but never come across, then your bridge is not doing its job. If your outreach is in fact not "bringing in" anyone – then close it and start something that is more effective!

I like the way the army does it. There is a river to be crossed, and there is a convoy of trucks waiting to go to the other side. They lay down a "Bailey Bridge" in about 4 hours flat. A simple bridge. But it does the job. I want to build "Bailey Bridge" ministries. I want to work out the simplest programme that will effectively bridge the gap and bring traffic across. The bridge has to go to the right place; it has to be strong enough to take the traffic; and it has to be attractive enough so that people will want to use it. **But I don't want to put any more effort into the bridge than that!**

We try to make Crossfire good enough so that non-Christian kids will want to use it to cross over to Jesus' side. But providing it is doing that job, I don't want to put any more effort into making it more and more attractive. God has not called me here to run magnificent youth programmes. He has called me here to bring people to him. If your bridge helps you do that – fantastic! If it doesn't, scrap it, re-read this whole book, and start again!

2. "Bringing In" Through Peer Witnessing

Whenever you mention an "evangelistic ministry" to a youth pastor, you can almost see their eyes light up. We youth pastors start dreaming big dreams. We see the vibrant outreach-oriented youth group at our church. We see the stadium full of repentant sinners streaming forward. We see smoke machines, outrageous activities, deafening music, and thousands upon thousands responding to **our** gospel message.

The first clue to effective outreach is "Don't necessarily think 'big programme'". Your most effective "bringing in" strategy is the personal witnessing of your high-school Christians. If you do not have a reasonable number of high-school Christians who are prepared to share their faith with their unsaved friends, there may be no value in planning a big outreach event. If your students are not doing the ministry for you – and it all depends on you and your adult leadership team, then you might not have very effective outreach at all.

We run a number of "Bringing In" activities at our church. We have our weekly youth group ("Crossfire"); we are involved in ministry at the local high school; we run evangelistic camps and hold special events. But the main reason that these activities produce "fruit that will last" is that we have an army of Christian high schoolers who are passionate to see their friends saved, and who will actively invite their friends along, and minister to them on the night.

So the starting point for effective evangelism might not be to start a big evangelistic event. It might not even be helpful to start a youth group! If you have a small youth ministry – with only a handful of Christian students involved, your starting point may well be to build up and disciple those Christian high-schoolers so that they are filled with a passion to reach their friends. When you have them actively praying for their friends and looking for ways to individually minister to them, I would almost be waiting for those young Christians to come back to me and say "Can we have some sort of activity where we can bring our unsaved friends that will help them to discover Jesus?" Then and only then would be the time to start an evangelistic youth group!

How do you get your Christian students passionate to reach out to their unsaved friends? You'll find most of the clues in Chapter 11, and the programme details in Chapter 15. Especially check out in Chapter 15 the information under "D-Teams" (Discipleship Teams). For practical ways to train students in effective personal ministry, see Chapter 16 – especially the "PEER Ministry Training" and "Evangelism Explosion".

3. "Bringing In" At Your Local High School

The local high school is of course the prime place that your Christian students can have an individual "Bringing In" ministry to their friends. But in a "programme" sense, there are many thing you can do to effectively reach students at their own high school.

a) Special Religious Education

Depending what country, state or territory you live in, there may well be the opportunity to teach the message of Jesus in your local State High School. You will need to check out the legal requirements where you live, but my comments are based on experience in the State Schools of New South Wales, Australia.

In NSW, legislation enables local Christian churches to have access to teaching the Christian faith in State Schools. Here are some clues to help make this ministry really effective:

i Design a system where both you and the school "win"

How the school timetables "Special Religious Education" ("Scripture") is a matter of negotiation between the local churches and the local school authorities. It depends on what sort of a timetable the school uses, how many personnel you have available as teachers, and how many students you want to reach. You can design an effective system when you have 10 Scripture teachers available, and you can design an effective system where you are the only person. Ask around, and talk to others who are doing it, and you will get some great clues. But don't end up with a system where the school "loses" (e.g. withdrawing some students every week from a Maths class so they fall behind in their school work); and don't end up with a system where you "lose" (e.g. having Scripture last period Friday, and students who don't do Scripture can go home early). Make sure you know your legal entitlements, but make sure you come up with a system that suits the school you are working in.

ii Build relationships with key staff.

You want to build solid relationships with students at your local schools? Well, first build relationships with some of the key staff. If you do not have the trust of the school staff, you will not have the opportunity to minister to students. If, for example, you have been given permission to talk with students in the schoolyard at lunchtime, then spend the first term going around to the staff rooms and getting to know the teachers. Your partnership with them will enable great relationships with students to develop later.

The principal and the deputy principal are obvious people to develop strong relationships with. Other people who might be able to be a great help to you are:

- The clerk at the front office
- The person in charge of the school timetable
- The person in charge of the school computer system

- The person in charge of the school printing room
- The General Assistant (plant manager, caretaker, handyman etc)
- The Teacher in charge of Welfare

iii Work hard at getting students "on your train"

If you walk into a classroom – ready to take a Scripture lesson – you probably have a firm idea of where you would like to lead those students to. You know that they are heading for an eternity without Christ – you want them to be following Jesus – and everything you do will attempt to lead them to that destination.

But there's no use charging off full-steam towards your destination if none of your students goes with you. Try and imagine yourself as a train driver with a mission to accomplish. You have to transport your students to a destination. You know what the destination is – and you are passionate to get them there. But no matter how keen you are – no matter how well you know your destination – and no matter how good a train driver you are, you will achieve nothing if you drive that train to your destination and leave all your "passengers" standing back at the platform!

Scripture at your local high school is as much about convincing your students to "get on your train", as it is about taking them to their destination. You know that you want to take them to Jesus. But they might not be convinced that that is where they want to go – and they might not trust you as a train driver.

I have no problem in spending 90% of a Scripture class helping students to see that it is worthwhile getting on the train, even if I only spend 10% of the time taking them there. There are plenty of other ministries that can help them make the journey.

iv Know what you want to achieve

Never lose sight of the fact that you want to win those students for Christ. In every series of lessons that I take with a class, I will want to give them an opportunity to tell me if they would like to become a Christian or take things further. I do this by enabling them to **write down** what their response is. I will usually have a lesson that calls for some written response that I will collect. When students know that I am the only other person who will read their response, they are usually prepared to be very honest. I then make sure I get back to them personally to chat about their response with them. For those who are genuine, there is then the opportunity to minister to them further, outside the constraints of a normal lesson.

But of course, not every student in your class will become a Christian. Realistically, many won't. But I still have definite aims I want to achieve with them. For those who don't take the step of submitting their life to Christ, I want to help them form the following three attitudes as a result of the time I have spent in the classroom with them.

- *Scripture is "okay"*
- *My Scripture Teacher is "okay"*
- *Jesus is "okay"*

If you can help students form these three attitudes, you are well on the way to taking them further along the path to discovering the difference that Jesus makes to their life.

v   Link in with other ministries

Do not teach "Scripture" in isolation. Use it as a springboard to usher students into further ministry opportunities. Use Scripture to invite students to the lunch-time Christian group at your school. Invite students to the youth ministry at your church. Invite them to special outreach events. Once I even organised an "after-school excursion" for my Year 7 Scripture Class. We met at a local hamburger restaurant, and then we went onto our Year 7 Youth Group. 15 students (half the class) came! The possibilities are endless.

One of the key ministries is to invite students to a 5 week "Discovering Jesus" Course. The details of "Discovering Jesus" are contained later in this chapter. But in every series of classes I take,

I will invite students to find out from the bible how to follow Jesus, by attending a "Discovering Jesus" course over 5 weeks – one lunchtime a week. This gives you an opportunity to develop strong relationships with interested students, and to help bring them to Christ in a more personal way.

b) Lunchtime Ministries

You may well have the opportunity of linking in with a lunchtime Christian group at your school. This can be a great way of supporting students who already attend your church, and contacting their friends who can be invited along. Good fellowship and partnership can be formed with students from other churches in your area. There may be the opportunity for special outreach events (concerts etc) at lunchtime. Check out what's possible. There are all sorts of "Bringing In" possibilities at your local school.

c) "Helping Out" Roles

Depending on your state legislation, there may be the opportunity for more informal contacts with students at your high school. Certainly, I have gone as a volunteer leader at school camps; I have been available for counselling in a crisis situation; I have served as a community representative on the School Council; I have been on an interview panel for a new Head Teacher; I have visited classes that are studying world religions to answer questions about Christianity; I have been a guest speaker at school functions. Others I know have helped coach school sports teams, assisted in remedial reading programmes, provided leadership training, and generally made themselves available to serve the school community. Currently "Crossfire" is a "gold sponsor" of our local high school. This means that one of our advertisements is in every school newsletter that goes home to parents. It simply makes sure our name is kept in everyone's sight.

Check out your local situation and see what ways there are to build links with your local High School community.

d) Placing a "staff" member at your high school

Depending on your state legislation, there may be the opportunity for local churches to combine to finance a full-time or part-time staff member to assist your local school. Such a person can help organise Scripture, liaise with the lunchtime Christian Group, and look for ways to get alongside both staff and students and we seek to draw people to Christ.

I believe this "Co-ordinator's" model outlined above is preferable to appointing a "Full-Time Scripture Teacher". If you have a "Full-Time Scripture Teacher" – who teaches all Scripture classes on behalf of local churches, you can easily lose the link that each individual church has with the local school. If you follow the "Co-ordinator's" role (as above), then among other things they **co-ordinate** the Scripture teaching by linking in with all the volunteers who come from local churches. If you can get enough volunteers to do this, it maintains a much stronger link between each local church and their local school.

e) "See You At The Pole"

The one ministry that has most grabbed my attention as a positive way of strengthening the Christian students at a high school, as well as providing a solid outreach to those around them is "See You at The Pole". Originating at Burleson High School, in Fort Worth, Texas, "See You At The Pole" simply means that on one morning of the year, Christian students show up an hour early at their school, and pray publicly for their school around their school flagpole. It is so simple. It is just a prayer meeting. But by doing it publicly, each Christian student makes a bold step to be publicly identified as a praying Christian, and the results have been hugely encouraging for everyone who has taken part. But the effect on the "onlookers" has been dramatic as well. Many witnessing situations have developed, and many schools use "See You at the Pole" to launch their ongoing ministries for the year.

I launched "See You at the Pole" in Australia in 1998. I simply challenged the Christians at our church as to whether they would be prepared to make this public stand at their high school, and to lead it themselves. I provided them with some basic resources, and the result a few weeks later was that 700 students prayed in 13 schools in our district. Praise God! The following year, with "word of mouth" advertising, about 1500 students prayed in about 40 schools.

What a great witness!

4. "Bringing In" At Your Church Youth Group

Once you have Christian students who are passionate about bringing their friends to Christ, you can have a superb ministry by focussing your youth group on reaching these new-comers.

Here is how we work things at "Crossfire":

a) General Principles

i   We divide into junior and senior high

It probably depends on your numbers as to whether you need 2 separate youth groups, but I would always advocate having separate ministries for junior and senior high. The needs of each are very different. Year 7s are just big kids, whereas Years 12 are about to enter the big bad world as adults.

We currently have 2 major youth groups. Years 6-8 (11-14 yr olds), and Years 9-12 (15-18 yr olds).

ii   We aim at the "first-timer"

We really want our Christian students to bring their friends to Crossfire. So we aim nearly everything we do at Crossfire at the newcomer. We want to make sure they feel welcomed. We want to make sure that they can understand what we're doing. We work hard to make Crossfire an "easy" place to drop into.

The test for any activity we are running, or for any segment of the night's programme is this: How will a first-timer react to that?

Indeed, just to make it a little more specific "How will a male student from a state school react to that?" If we work out it would be difficult for a first-timer to get involved, we probably won't do it.

iii We proclaim Jesus from the Scriptures

We want to send the message that everything we do centres around Jesus. We want to show that it is God's word that provides the only answers for our life. So every week, we have a message about Jesus which comes straight from the bible. Yes – we try to be creative. Yes - we want to apply this in a way that is relevant. Yes - we want to hit the issues that are on the hearts of our young people. But every week the message is about Jesus. Because every week is aimed at the first-timer. There is never a wrong week to bring your friends.

b) What does a night look like?

Given that every week is a bit different, and junior high is different from senior high, what does an average night at Crossfire look like? Here is how a typical night might go at "Crossfire X" (Years 9-12 at high school) Where there is a significant variation for Junior High, it will be noted. (Junior High operates 2 hours earlier than the time here)

i   8:00 – 8:25 pm – "Hang Time"
Developing Casual Relationships

The first half hour is intentionally designed for students to "hang around". This works well in our culture where students have a lot of structured demands placed on them during the week. The aim of this time is to enable students to relax in an unstructured setting, and catch up with each other. This is the ideal time for our Adult Leadership team to get alongside students and build relationships.

Even though this time is "unstructured', there are still plenty of things for students to do. We have some skating equipment set up in a roped-off section of the carpark, and a number of students will be skating there with one or two leaders. We have a portable basketball ring set up in the courtyard. A small room has a portable PA and some flashing lights and is our "Dance Party" Room – music at high volumes! In another small room we have a computer games console hooked up to a video projector – where 4 players can interact on the big screen. We have a "Snack Shack" selling drinks and confectionery. We have a pool table, a couple of pinball machines, and a few other assorted entertainment devices. These are just scattered around the available halls on our church property, and they give the student who is "looking" for something to do, the opportunity to be involved.

If you have a smaller youth ministry, you do not need a "big budget" to set up something like this. You can simply start with equipment owned by leaders in your group. The principle is the same – provide a "structure" so that students can be "unstructured". We find that many many students just want to stand around and catch up with each other. This is an ideal time for leaders to build relationships!

From the point of view of a newcomer, they arrive at the group and they don't "have" to do anything immediately, Whether they arrive early or late, they can hang around with their friends in a very low-key setup. We are aiming that "Hang Time" will have the effect on a newcomer of helping them to feel "This is a cool place. I'm glad I'm here!"

It also means that if parents have arrived with their children for the first time, that some of our leaders can chat with the parents while their teenagers go off and join in these passive activities. This is particularly true at our junior high group!

The Junior High Group would have less activities available in their opening "Hang Time" and would probably have no longer than 15 minutes of unstructured time in one hit.

ii 8:25 – 8:35 Whole Group Celebration & Welcome
Developing "Big Group" Community

We gather everyone together in our main meeting area (which at the moment is our church - with all the seats pushed back so there is a large carpeted area on the floor). As students walk in, the music is going – sometimes we have some video from a Crossfire Camp on the big screen – the aim is for the place to be "alive" and "happening" from the word "go".

A leader will welcome the crowd from out the front, and we will try to present things in a high-energy way so that the newcomer might feel "This is the place to be. I'm glad I'm here". We will try and "build" the programme for the night – and give students a taste of where we are going to head. We might do something crazy out the front (3 students playing a game that involves a cream pie), or we might honour one of our students who has just achieved something great in sport, academic studies, performing arts etc.

This section of the programme is "brief", but for many it will be their first experience of "being together", so we try to make it very positive.

Our junior high group (with their shorter hang time), might have a longer "Celebration and Welcome", and may involve a number of "whole group" games.

iii 8:35 – 8:55 Smaller Community Time
Developing Real Community in a Smaller Setting

Because our youth groups have large numbers (100 – 200 each group), we intentionally break it down into smaller communities of less than 50. (If your whole youth group is still small, this step might not be so vital). We divide into "Year Groups at School". So in our Senior High Group, we have a Year 9 Group, a Year 10 group, a Year 11 group, and a Year 12 group. Junior High works the same.

Here is why we do this:

- In smaller groups (about 50) each student can get a much better feeling of "really belonging", rather than just being part of a huge crowd all the time.
- We have leaders permanently assigned to each age group. That means that leaders can get to know the same group of students each week, and start building helpful relationships with them.
- The leaders for each "Year Group" are under the direction of a "Year Co-ordinator". The person who is the Year Co-ordinator takes responsibility for all ministry to that age group (not just Crossfire, but also D-teams etc). It is this team of "Year Co-ordinators" who ensure that we have appropriate ministry across all age groups.

What we do in each Year Group will vary depending on the age of the students. But normally, each week 20 – 30 minutes will be spent in these separate year groups, doing things which are appropriate for that age. (Year 6s play a lot of games! Year 12 play very little!!)

But the aims for each Year Group are the same:
- To build an identity as a smaller Year Group
- To welcome the newcomers
- To start students thinking about where we are heading that night

We want students to feel not just "I'm a part of the Crossfire Community", but also "I'm a part of this Year 10 Group". We want students to take some ownership for the "success" of their Year Group, and be passionate to invite more and more to come along.

In these Year Groups we will normally have some short exercise to help students to mingle with each other, and then we will always ask "Who met someone who is here at Crossfire for the very first time?" Regular students then introduce their "guest", and each one is roundly applauded and cheered by the whole group.

Note that we get the **regular** students to introduce the newcomers. We don't ask newcomers to identify themselves by asking "Well, who's new?" We want to welcome our newcomers in a way that is genuine and wholehearted, without being threatening.

We have a small gift which we present to each "first-time guest" individually. We have a plastic sports bottle with our logo emblazoned on it, and inside this we put pamphlets and other information about our ministries. We also usually include a small packet of confectionery! This is our way of saying "welcome" to each new-comer, and giving them something tangible to express our appreciation for showing up.

We give each "newcomer" a "Guest card" to fill in, so we have a record of who has visited. We then mail that person a "Thank you" note during the week, and send them a voucher which they can redeem at our Snack Shack" in the next 2 weeks for a free can of drink or a free chocolate. We do this as a "little extra" to help turn "First-Time Visitors" into "Second-Time Visitors". We find that students who come along at least twice, are much more likely to keep coming than students who only come along once.

Of course, our newcomers keep those "Welcome Bottles" with them throughout the night, which means in the "Hang –Time" after Crossfire, it is very easy to spot who the newcomers are! I always make a bee-line to go over and talk with them!

We make a big feature of welcoming newcomers, and we always expect that in every year group every week there will be new people. Of course, this only happens because our Christian students are actively praying for and inviting their friends!

We will also try and **build community** in this Year Group. Depending on the age, anything from playing games, doing trust exercises, talking about current school issues, watching a video, or even cooking pancakes might happen during this time! It is up to the Year Co-ordinator and their team of leaders to programme this part of the night.

Sometimes we will have **discussion questions** or other interactive activities to help students start thinking about one of the issues that will be preached on later. We want to do everything we can so that God's word will be the most impactful it can be on the night!

iv 8:55 – 9:05 – Creative Ministry
   Asking the Questions that God's Word will Answer

When we gather all the year Groups back together again, we "re-introduce" Crossfire with a short segment of "Creative Ministry". This section is normally taken by one of our "Discipleship Teams". They will be given the task – maybe a month ahead of the scheduled date - to come up with some "Creative Ministry" that will help everyone to start thinking about the issues that the preacher is going to tackle.

We encourage students to use a variety of media in this. Sometimes they will shoot their own video – or use a video clip that deals with the issue. Some groups sing, or dance, or use drama. or a game, and often one or more of the students will share their testimony. We encourage variety – and a good presentation will have a combination of many of the above suggestions.

At the end of the Creative Ministry, we want students to already be thinking about the issue that the preacher is going to tackle. So by the time the preacher stands up the front, we want the first-timer to be thinking "So far – so good!"

v 9.05 – 9.25 – Preaching
   Proclaiming Christ from the Scriptures

Because our target at Crossfire is the new-comer ... because our aim is evangelism, then every week, we preach about Jesus. That is exactly what the new-comer needs to hear about. That is precisely what will challenge the unbeliever to start exercising saving faith.

We started in 1993 by preaching our way through John's gospel. We would simply take the next "bit", and preach on the issues it raised. It always took us straight to Jesus, but we also discovered that it really hit the spot as far as dealing with issues that are real for teenagers today. We tried varying this for a while, and talked about issues such as "Sexuality". "Coping with Parents" "Drugs and Alcohol" and other "hot" youth topics. While we found that these were helpful issues, they did not take us anywhere near the gospel, and we saw fewer students saved. So after this short detour, we returned to John's gospel , and two and half years laster we finished it! Then we took a further two and a half years going through Luke's gospel - and now we've started John all over again!

We aim for our preaching to be punchy; to be concise; to be funny; to be relevant; to be powerful. But above all we aim that our message will proclaim the power of Christ, and challenge our students to respond in repentance and faith.

The conclusion of the sermon is normally something like ..."Think about it. Work out if you're ready to change your life for Jesus. Come and talk with us in the 'Chat Room'" (see below). About once a term, we will challenge students in the whole group to make a decisions for Christ right there on the spot.

Junior High gets the same message as Senior High. The same preacher will usually do both groups. With Junior High we will change the illustrations to be more appropriate to that age group. And sometimes the overall message will be a little shorter. But it is basically the same

vi 9.25 – 9.30 – Final Wrap Up
Reinforcing the Message and Inviting to Return

We have a short spot after the message to bring everything to a conclusion. The aim of this segment is to re-inforce the message that has just been proclaimed, and invite students to ask further questions in the "Chat Room". It is also our opportunity to advertise anything that we want to encourage our students to be involved with. And we want to issue a warm invitation for students to return the following week when the Crossfire Community gathers once more.

With our Junior High Group, this section may be a little longer, and we might include a final "all together" game, or other stunt.

vi 9:30 – 10:00 – Final Hang Time
Intentional Relationship Developing

The final half hour is very similar to the opening "Hang Time". All the activities listed there will appear again. But there are two new factors in this final time of developing relationships:

- **The Chat Room.**
  We establish a "Chat Room" for the final Hang Time. It is simply a small lounge area, that has a couple of our "Evangelism Explosion" teams in attendance. We want to establish a culture so that students always know there is somewhere they can go and hassle through issues in their life. There is always somewhere where they can ask further questions about following Jesus.

  It is an incredible concept that our own Christian students can be available to help their non-Christian friends discover the difference that Jesus can make to their lives. But that is the value of our "Evangelism Explosion" ministry. Every week there is the opportunity for students to come to the "Chat Room" and to go "one step further" in their relationship with Jesus.

- **Welcoming newcomers**
  We have already welcomed newcomers in our programme. But the final hang-time is an opportunity for all leaders to catch up with those who have come for the first time. Certainly as the youth pastor, I will be on the lookout for new students - to try and establish a relationship with them.

  And how do we "spot" the newcomers? Simple, really. If one of our regular students doesn't come and introduce them to us, we find them pretty quickly because they're carrying around one of our Crossfire Sports Bottles!

With our Junior High Group, the final "Hang Time" is usually a little shorter – often about 15 – 20 minutes.

That's roughly what a Crossfire Night looks like. Sometimes we switch things around. Sometimes we will have different times on these things. Some nights we will do something special and crazy. But really this is the sort of programme that anyone could run . It is simply an opportunity to create a place where Christian students feel confident to bring their unsaved friends, knowing that we will challenge them with the message of Jesus.

To borrow an expression from Bill Hybels - we want Crossfire to be "a safe place to hear a dangerous message".

5. "Bringing In" Through "Discovering Jesus"

a) The Birth of "Discovering Jesus"

Many years ago, we had a large and vibrant Year 8 Youth Group. About 80-90 students would come along every week. A good leadership team was attempting to share God's word with this dynamic and noisy crowd. Despite our best efforts, and despite the apparent "success" of the group, we were finding it was very hard to get to the students who were showing some response to Jesus.

We needed a better strategy. How do we take the interested students "one step further"? How do we complete the "Bringing In" strategy so that we might take some students all the way to the cross of Jesus, and then start the "Building Up" process in their life?

"What if we offered a one hour bible study before Crossfire for 5 weeks? Do you think interested students would show up?"

It was worth a shot. We advertised it for a few weeks. We advertised it as "One hour of bible study to find out what it really means to follow Jesus. No games, no activities, just one hour of studying the bible". We were serious about weeding out the interested students who were ready to make a step for Jesus.

The result? **32 students put their names down!** We were suddenly faced with the dilemma – What bible studies are we going to use? What bible studies are appropriate for junior high, designed for students who are not necessarily Christians, and will take students through the gospel and challenge them to make a decision to respond?

The search of the local Christian Bookstores was fruitless. It looked like we would have to write our own. In the weeks that followed, "Discovering Jesus" was born!

b) The Strategy of "Discovering Jesus"

"Discovering Jesus" is a booklet of 5 short bible studies, which is aimed to be easily readable by junior highs (although we use it for senior high as well!). It is designed for use by both Christians and non-Christians, and the aim is to take students through the gospel, and to show them from the bible what a decision to follow Jesus truly involves. The studies are simple to follow, and are short enough so that you can complete them in a school lunchtime if necessary.

The 5 studies in the book are:
1. Discovering God
2. Discovering Me
3. Discovering Jesus
4. Discovering Jesus' Death
5. Discovering My Response

Here is why the "Discovering Jesus" ministry is so crucial in our strategy of "making disciples":

> i *It finds the students who are wanting to find out more*

We consistently offer "Discovering Jesus" to those students who are wanting to go further. It is a turning point, in that it enables us to progress from "generally evangelising the whole crowd" to "specifically evangelising the smaller number who are really interested".

ii It helps students to decide to follow Jesus

Many many students have started "Discovering Jesus" because they were interested to find out more – and have gone on to make a commitment because of what they learned in the course. A large number of students in our ministry at Crossfire have come to real faith in Christ through the ministry of "Discovering Jesus".

iii It's the first follow up to those who have made a commitment

When we challenge students to make a commitment to Christ – at Crossfire, or on a camp, then "Discovering Jesus" is the first structured form of follow-up that we offer. The same is true if we get a referral from a large rally like "Youth Alive". It enables us to take students carefully through the gospel so that they can be certain about the step that they are taking to follow Jesus with their life.

iv It reassures the young Christian

We make "Discovering Jesus" the **first** small group that we plug any Christian student into. If a high-schooler wants to join a "Discipleship Team" (Home Bible Study Group), then we ask them to complete a 5 week "Discovering Jesus" Course first. By taking them through the gospel again, it reassures the young Christian in their faith. And of course, some of the "Christian" students who start "Discovering Jesus" realise that they're not really a Christian – and subsequently make an informed and real commitment!

v It's the beginning of our "Discipleship Team" Ministry

The heart and soul of our youth ministry is our Discipleship Teams (explained in detail in Chapter 15). This is where the main work of "making disciples" occurs. The overwhelming majority of students who complete a 5 week "Discovering Jesus" Course go on to be part of a permanent Discipleship Team.

vi It's the turning point from "Bringing In" to "Building Up"

I believe the crucial ministries in your strategy are the ones that help you "turn the corner" from one level of ministry to the next. You will see from our Ministry Strategy Diagram in the appendix that we have 3 crucial "turning point" ministries. "Discovering Jesus" is one of them, because it completes the "Bringing In" ministry for a student, and commences them on the "Building Up" ministry.

c) The Programming of "Discovering Jesus"

Very simple, really. We keep advertising "Discovering Jesus" at Crossfire. We advertise it through "Scripture" at the local High School. We invite students to commit themselves for 5 weeks to find out from the bible how to follow Jesus. We will particularly offer this after we have had a large evangelistic ministry. We will often offer these course so they are directly before or after Crossfire (or before or after Church). This often makes it easier for students to attend (and one less trip their parents need to make in the family car!) At school, we can do them at lunchtimes

As soon as we have a handful of students ready to go, we get one of our leaders to start a group. We divide by gender (separate boys' groups from girls' group – we find it works a whole lot better!) and we have different junior high groups from senior high groups. Where possible we will run a Discovering Jesus group for a specific Year Group only (e.g. year 7 girls' group). The advantage of this is if the whole group wants to go on to become a permanent Discipleship Team, then they are "ready to go" – often with the original leader.

At the end of the 5 weeks, the leader will catch up with each student individually and help them assess what the next step will be. Some students simply do the 5 weeks, and work out that they're not really interested. But the overwhelming majority will either have just become Christians, or be strengthened in their faith, which will result in either the whole Discovering Jesus Group progressing to become a permanent Discipleship Team, or that those who have come out of a Discovering Jesus Group will then be transplanted into existing Discipleship Teams.

Chapter 14
Programming For "Building Up"

The "Building Up" Ministry is so crucial. It describes the vast bulk of ministry you will do with a person once they have taken the step to place their trust in Jesus. At our church there are many components to our "building up" ministry. It starts with the immediate follow-up ministry that we have with a student just after they make a commitment to follow Jesus. "Building Up" includes our church services, which are primarily aimed at our believers – to strengthen them for their life and ministry. We run a week-long camp in the Christmas School Holidays aimed at building up our high school believers (described in Chapter 16).

But the key "programme" to "building up" disciples is our weekly "D-Teams" (Discipleship Teams). Other churches might call them "Bible Study Groups" or "Home Fellowship Groups" or "Growth Groups" or whatever. I believe that groups like this are the key to not only "building up" disciples, but also have the potential to help you to turn the corner in your strategy and start the passion for "sending out".

1. The Importance of D-Teams

If you came along to look at our youth ministry, you would probably conclude that "Crossfire" on Friday Nights was they main thing that we ran. It gets the largest numbers, it makes the most noise, and it breaks the most windows!

"Crossfire" is certainly central to what we do … but it is not our main ministry. The heart and soul of our ministry actually lies in our D-Teams.

Why is this?

FRUIT THAT WILL LAST

"Crossfire" is our shop-front evangelistic ministry. It is where masses of students discover Jesus and are saved. But the **reason** that we see a fruitful ministry at Crossfire is because of our "D-Team" Ministry. Not only do our D-team students help run part of the Crossfire programme, but the main reason that masses of newcomers visit Crossfire, and the main reason why our evangelistic messages at Crossfire are so fruitful is because "Crossfire" is the opportunity for our D-team students who have been "sent out" into their schools to have a "bringing in" ministry back on our turf.

Our best form of evangelism ministry – is not Crossfire – but the training of Christian students to be passionate witnesses in our D-team ministry. If for some reason there was a law passed that said we were only allowed to run **one** ministry – and one ministry **only** – we would close down everything else and still run our D-teams. If we closed down Crossfire – but we kept our D-teams going – evangelism would still happen - and students would still be saved!

This is not putting down the ministry of Crossfire! It is huge – and I love it! It is simply showing how crucial our D-teams really are.

A D-Team is a group of Christian high-schoolers who want to grow together as disciples, and be trained as disciple-makers. It is a discipleship team which grows together under the guidance of a coach so that they can impact the world for Christ.

D-Teams are where students are cared for...where disciples are grown...where missionaries are trained...where ministries are birthed...and where the world is changed. They are the central catalyst for everything we do.

2. How To Get Started

a) How We Start New Groups

The overwhelming majority of our D-teams start as "Discovering Jesus" Groups (discussed in the previous chapter). We challenge students to do a 5 week "Discovering Jesus" Course to find out from the bible what it means to follow Jesus. As students make a commitment to be a disciple of Jesus, we invite them to continue on in a permanent D-Team.

b) How We Got Our Name

We struggled for some time with what to call our "D-Teams". In the good old days we had always called them "Bible Study Groups". That was an okay name because it kept our focus on God's Word. But the reason we looked for a change was that the name "Bible Study Group" didn't describe **why** the group met. It simply described one of our activities.

Ultimately, we didn't meet for the purpose of studying the bible. We met so we would grow as disciples and be trained as disciple-makers. Yes - studying the bible was central to this, but we also prayed, held each other accountable, shared our joys and sorrows together, worshipped God together and strengthened each other in fellowship.

The name "Home Fellowship" was a strong possibility, but once again, this didn't describe the reason why we met. Sure – good fellowship did happen among us – but we didn't meet for the purpose of having fellowship. Fellowship was the natural result of Christians growing together as disciples. "Discipleship Group" seemed like a better alternative.

Why "Team" and not "Group"? "Team" seemed to better catch the biblical concept of the body. We are a team of individuals who together act in unity to achieve a result. The word "group" only seemed to catch up the idea of a collection of people jumbled together. "Team" immediately conjured up pictures of sporting teams where each individual works with the whole group to produce a successful outcome. So "Discipleship Teams" (or D-Teams for short) were born.

(Okay – all of you who have visited Willow Creek will know that we are not the only church in the world to call our small groups "D-Teams". When I chatted with Bo Boshers at Willow Creek, and he explained his "Delta Teams" (D-Teams for short), the name "D-Team" seemed to catch on easily. There is nothing new under the sun! Thank you, Bo!)

c) Where we get our D-Team "Coaches" from

Our coaches (or leaders) of our D-Team have normally started out with us as Crossfire leaders on a Friday Night. We encourage all our Crossfire leaders to pray that God will raise up some of their students who will want to do "Discovering Jesus". That Crossfire leader then takes on the Discovering Jesus group as a short term project. If the Discovering Jesus Group goes on to become a permanent D-Team, then their leader will probably move on with them.

So we keep losing our Crossfire leaders as they become D-Team Coaches! Every year we need to replace our Crossfire leaders with brand new leaders. We never have enough! But somehow God manages to keep us going!

But the principle for our leaders in this setup is this: We start our brand new leaders in the large Crossfire Group – where their ministry is supervised, and where they have the advantage of belonging to a specified team which meets together each week. Then, as that leader matures and grows, sometimes they move on to the more specialised ministry of a "D-Team", where they will have a little less supervision and need to be a little more resourceful.

3. How To Organise D-teams

a) When we meet

In a programme sense, our D-Teams operate in a decentralised way. They meet at a time and a place that suits the leader and the students involved. Most meet in the houses of the members – others meet at our church facilities. A number of our D-Teams meet before or after church, or before or after Crossfire. But the rest meet at whatever time of the week is suitable.

There's nothing wrong with organising this in a more centralised way. I know of many places that have all their small groups on a Sunday afternoon or a Tuesday evening. We used to operate our small groups on

Sunday afternoon before church. We would all meet together – we would have a time of singing and prayer – something inspirational from "out the front" – and then we would divide up into our small groups.

Why did we make the change? Simply to change the dynamics. By having all our small groups meeting together on Sunday, it felt like "another youth group". It seemed to the students that we were asking them to commit to two separate youth groups - Crossfire on Friday Night, and "Combined Small Groups" on Sunday afternoon. By changing to "decentralised" groups, it helped us to ask our core Christian students to make a three-fold commitment:

i   Celebrate and grow with the whole body at Church each Sunday (Large group – about 400)

ii   Be personally discipled and supported in your D-Team (Small group of 6-8)

iii Have a ministry to your friends at Crossfire (Medium Group – 100-150)

b) Our Study Material

We give our D-teams reasonable autonomy in what they study. There is no centralised obligatory curriculum. Here's the thinking behind that. The **key** to producing "fruit that will last" in our D-Teams is the discipling relationship between the D-Team Coach and his students. The main way that we uphold high standards in the ministry of our D-Teams is to make sure that we're upholding a high standard in the life of each D-Team Coach. As long as we have the **right** person sowing God's word into the lives of our students, then we know that we will produce good fruit.

However, we do have a **recommended** path for our D-Teams to follow.

i   For Junior High

I have written a series of bible study books aimed at building disciples of junior highs. The series is called "Growing Young Disciples" and it takes junior highs through the basics of being a faithful disciple, and an effective disciple-maker.

The books in this series are:

- *"Discovering Jesus"*
  Introductory book to help students know for sure that they are following Jesus (explained in detail in Chapter 13)
- *"First Steps"*
  Introduces students to bible reading, prayer, and the other basics of Christian growth.
- *"Second Thoughts"*
  Helps young disciples to deal with doubts
- *"Life to the Max"*
  Helps young disciples to enjoy living "flat out" for Jesus
- *"How To Really Stick At Being A Christian"*
  Helps young disciples to stick at following Jesus by taking them through Peter's first letter

These books are published by "CEP", and should be available at your local Christian bookstore. Each book contains five studies.

ii For Senior High

Often at about the beginning of Year 10, we ask students if they are ready to give a 3 year commitment to their D-team. That is, we want them to stay in the same D-team, with hopefully the same coach until the end of Year 12 (when they will leave school). This commitment enables them to be thoroughly trained in all the essential building blocks which will establish them as life-time disciples and passionate disciple-makers.

The series is called "Discipleship Training", and I am hopeful it will be published **real soon!**

The books in the series are:

- *"My New Life"*
  Helps you to have the absolute fundamentals of being a disciple and a disciple-maker operating in your day to day life.

- *"My Awesome God"*
  Introduces you to the majesty of a relationship with God as your Father, Jesus as your Lord, and the indwelling power of God's Holy Spirit.

- *"My Intimate Relationship"*
  Helps you to deepen your relationship with God through immersing yourself in his Word, and in prayer.

- *"My Mission From God"*
  Trains you in the day to day ministry of being both a faithful steward, and an effective witness.

- *"My Personal Obedience"*
  Helps each disciple to honour Jesus in their personal life in very practical ways

Each book contains ten studies.

4. The Role of the "Coach"

a) The concept of a D-Team "coach"

We use the term "coach" for the leader of each D-team to continue the sporting imagery. The picture of a sporting coach is a good one to help us understand the role of a "pastor". The coach does not try to make all the plays in a game while the team members just watch – but by setting the example himself he equips others to be the players and enjoy the victories. The coach trains individuals – but also helps the whole team to play as a unit. The coach cheers enthusiastically from the sidelines, and makes any corrections which are necessary as the game progresses.

We don't want our D-Team Coaches to do all the ministry themselves. We want them to train and equip their students to develop their own ministry for a lifetime.

A dictionary definition of a coach might read this way " a person who trains athletes for G.A.M.E.S. or contests" (you'll see why we have highlighted the word "G.A.M.E.S" a little later). The bible defines the role of a pastor or shepherd (or coach!) in these terms:

"... some to be pastors and teachers, to prepare God's people for works of service, so that the body of Christ may be built up"
Ephesians 4: 11-12

To paraphrase Ephesians 4: 11-2, a D-Team Coach prepares students for a lifetime of ministry so that the whole body of believers keeps growing.

b) The Commitment of a D-Team Coach

To be an effective discipler, we ask our D-team coaches to make the following commitment:

Here is your commitment:	Specifically this means:
You need to commit yourself to constant growth in your own walk with God.	As well as growing in godliness and obedience in every area of your life, you will need to double check your own faithfulness in these key areas: a) Consistency and growth in your own personal quiet times b) A life of active ministry to those around you c) Regular, weekly attendance at our church services at St. Paul's d) Biblical and sacrificial giving to the support of God's work e) Being involved in your own ongoing bible study group where you are being ministered to and fed. f) Absolute discretion and godliness in your relationships with the opposite sex.
You need to commit yourself to consistent and regular prayer for those whom you are training.	Maintain a prayer list for your group to keep yourself on track in praying for them regularly.

Here is your commitment:	Specifically this means:
You need to prepare thoroughly for your weekly D-Team.	Commit your D-Team to regular prayer so that by the time you actually meet, every step of the way has been bathed in prayer. Go through the bible passages carefully, and work out your main teaching points, and specific points of application.
You need to meet faithfully and regularly with those whom you are discipling, and teach them God's word in a way that has real impact on their life.	Normally you will need to meet weekly, with breaks each term for holidays etc.
You need to model and show the practicalities of everything you teach, and hold your group accountable to you and to each other to continue in what they have learnt.	Make sure you feel confident in the areas that you are to teach. Simply show your group the way you do things, and get them to copy you. Once they have learnt your way, encourage them to develop their own style in everything they do.
You need to commit yourself to these young people as your prime ministry commitment.	a) While you are a D-Team Coach, this will be the main ministry that you have. Other things might have to go to make way for it. b) You need to commit yourself to each young person outside your normal group time. **Every Week** • Make some personal contact with EVERY student individually in your group - by a quick phone call, talking after church etc

Here is your commitment:	Specifically this means:
	• Spend some significant time with ONE member of your group. You might spend a couple of hours together - perhaps involve them in things you are doing - but spend time - chat - listen - this is where huge ministry will occur
You need to have a ministry to the parents of your students.	Make regular contact - by phone, in person, with all parents of your students - both Christian and non-Christian. Not only will this strengthen the ministry a family can have but it will help parents trust what you are doing with their child.
You need to be accountable to your pastor for everything you are doing as a D-Team leader.	Stay in close contact with your Year Co-ordinator - and be open to seeking help and guidance, and keep giving information and feedback as to how things are going for you.

5. How to keep your D-teams on track

By allowing our D-Teams to operate in a decentralised way, we need to have some method of ensuring that each D-team is meeting their ministry objectives. We have developed the "G.A.M.E.S" method of evaluating each group.

Here are 5 key questions that each D-Team Coach needs to keep asking about the ministry of their group:

G **Growth**
Are the members of our team growing in Christ?
Is there kingdom growth because of our D-Team?

A **Accountability**
Are we honest with each other in our D-Team?
Do we hold each other accountable as disciples?

M **Ministry**
Are we exercising a ministry to St Paul's & Crossfire?
Are we ministering to individuals outside our team?

E **Equipping**
Am I training our team in personal Christlikeness?
Am I equipping our team for ministry in the world?

S **Support**
Do we genuinely love and care for each other?
Do we model God's grace in accepting and supporting each other?

By constantly asking these questions, each D-team Coach is able to determine whether their group is achieving the results we are looking for in the essential "building up" ministry of our D-teams.

6. How to keep your Coaches on track

There are thousands of things that a D-team Coach could be doing with their D-Team. But by using the "G.A.M.E.S." guidelines, each coach can be helped to focus on the essentials so that we do indeed raise up an army of committed disciples who are prepared for a lifetime of enthusiastic disciple-making ministry.

Because we are committed to:		At your weekly D-Team meetings, you will:	And outside your normal group time, you will:
G	**Growth**	• Study God's Word • Encourage bible memorisation • Pray with passion • Worship God with awe	• Aim to spend some sustained time together in Christian growth. (weekend away, a day to have an extended time of bible study, prayer, sharing, worship etc. together
A	**Account-ability**	• Share individually with each other how we're going. • Discuss how to apply the Scriptures personally. • Discuss about how God has been speaking to each person and answering prayer through individual quiet times. • Challenge each other to personal godliness and growth • Discuss how "church" is going (attendance, involvement, growth, learning) • Spur one another on to love and good works!	• Catch up with students individually to hold each one accountable in specific areas • Discuss how to apply the Scriptures personally. • Discuss how God has been speaking to each person and answering prayer through individual quiet times.
M	**Ministry**	• Continue to pray for each other's "3 unsaved friends" • Actively encourage students in their Peer Witnessing at School • Plan for your organised ministry at Crossfire (Creative Ministry, Cleaning Up etc)	• Hold an outreach event for the students to bring their friend to. (e.g. have a dinner with speaker /video /discussion etc) • Hold an event aimed at the parents of your group members. (Parents' Appreciation" dinner./outreach dinner etc.).. • Be involved in a service project together - help cleaning at church, babysit for church couples, help collect, fold pamphlets etc.

The table header spans: "Then the D-Team Coach will make sure that:"

E	Equipping	• Plan how to use "Crossfire" or other outreach ministries to intentionally reach our friends • Discuss ministry opportunities that occurred during the week • Train students in how to share their faith • Train students in how to care for each other.	• Involve individual students in specific ministry training with you • Come along to Crossfire, and train your students by example in how to welcome, befriend, and evangelise other students.
S	Support	• Work hard at listening to each other • Model genuine care and love within the group • Support and "bind up the wounds" of those who are hurting • Reach out to team members who are falling away • Have a time to relax - chat, wrestle, whatever. Have munchies for supper, etc. • Do some exercises that will encourage group trust and openness	• Spend individual time with each student. Care for them as an individual • Spend some social time together.

7. Now tell me again, why does this really matter?

We put so much emphasis on this "Building Up" Ministry, because this is where we will train high-schoolers for a lifetime of active and passionate ministry. If we want to see "fruit that will last", then the hard work we put in at this stage will be absolutely crucial.

The ministry of "D-teams" is so important because it is the turning point for moving from our "Building Up" strategy to our "Sending Out" strategy. For it is in a D-Team that students will begin to discover the passion for reaching out to their unsaved friends, and having a ministry of support and encouragement to fellow believers.

Because the aim of our D-teams is to train disciples for a lifetime of future ministry, and the key factor in this is the relationship between the D-team coach and their handful of students, then where possible, we will often keep the same coach with the same students for a number of years. This doesn't always work out – and sometimes it is right for a change, but we generally look at the ministry of a D-team coach as spanning a number of years.

This ministry really is worth it!

> I can remember a few years ago when I sat down with a number of Year 7 boys who were just starting "Discovering Jesus". They were interested – but they were restless. They fidgeted. They fought. They flatulated. It was a constant battle to keep them on track. But I genuinely loved each one, and sought to sow into them a passion to be strong for Jesus and to infiltrate a world that was dying. I wanted them to love following Jesus – to love serving in the body - and to love their unsaved friends enough to bring them to Christ.

> Three years later as I write this, they are now in Year 10. They are all still there, and they are all still growing in Christ. Many of them have had the joy of seeing at least one of their friends whom they have been praying for give his life to Christ. They are learning how to share with others the faith that they have. They still get restless. They still fidget. They still fight. They still flatulate. But they are growing in Christ, and I am aiming to start them on a lifetime of worship and service – so they will indeed be "fruit that will last".

> Sometimes I feel like I am getting nowhere. And then God has his own way of encouraging me. One of my Year 10s slipped me a note a few weeks ago. Here is a short except:

> *"... You have Jesus running through your blood and he shows through you ... I always think of where I would be in my life without you as I would have found Christianity very hard ... thanks for being so caring as a coach, a brother in Christ, and a friend. ..."*

> I believe this story is repeated time and time again amongst our D-Team Coaches as they sow into young lives to "Build Them Up" and "Send Them Out".

> Specifically, how do we train our students and "send them out" for active ministry?

> Read on!

Chapter 15
Programming For "Sending Out"

Congratulations on making it this far! By the time you get to this chapter in the book, you might have forgotten where it all started. Programming for "Sending Out" is vital because it is this "Sending Out" that is the very reason that Jesus has left us here on the planet. God is calling upon you – and your leadership team – and your high-school disciples – to go and make a difference in the world that desperately needs him.

It's no use telling your students that they should "go out and minister" unless you equip them and train them and show them how to do it.

Hang on to your hats! This is exciting stuff!

There are three main areas where you need to have good programming for "Sending Out". Here are some programming ideas to get your creative juices flowing!

1. Train Every Student to Minister

Whilst every D-team should be inspiring and equipping each high-school disciple for a lifetime of active ministry, we want to provide specific training so that **every** young disciple – whether they ever become a "youth leader" or not – is equipped in the two key areas of "Peer Care" and "Peer Witnessing".

We have not yet developed our specific training for "Peer Care" (still under construction!) But there are our two main programmes to train students for "Peer Witnessing"

a) PEER Ministry Training Course

This is a course which we are still developing, but then idea is to enable

D-Teams to specifically prepare each of their students for active peer ministry.

Here is an outline of the course:

i. How to be a player on Jesus' team

Outcomes of this unit:
- Students will understand, and be excited by, the vision for being players, not spectators, on Jesus' team.
- Students will understand our ministry plan and their role in it.
- Students will be looking for ways to put this ministry into action.
- Students will know our purpose, mission and strategy by memory.

Content of this Unit:
- We will teach the biblical importance of being active in ministry.
- Students will discover the vital place that Jesus has for them on his team.
- We will introduce themto the "why" of Crossfire - our vision, purpose, mission and strategy.

Comments:

The whole thrust of this study is to show students that when Jesus calls them to follow him, he also calls them onto his ministry team. He doesn't want us to be "spectators", he wants us to be "players". To help them have a ministry that centres around Crossfire, we ask them to memorise the 3 Vision Statements so they know precisely what we believe God wants Crossfire to achieve. You will find a copy of these statements in the Appendix.

ii How to Develop the Jesus HABITS.

Outcomes of this unit:
- Students will understand the importance of their own personal walk, and not to be dependent on a programme to keep them faithful.

- Students will have started to put the HABITS into operation in their own life - with joy!
- Students will have a ready accountability for introducing any remaining habits in the short-term future.

Content of this Unit:

- We will focus on the importance of developing the habits of personal faithfulness - so that your growth as a Christian is not dependent on a programme, or on a personality, but on the person of Jesus.
- We will teach the specific lifelong development of the following 6 HABITS:

At this point can I commend the ministry of Doug Fields – who in his excellent book "Purpose Driven Youth Ministry" outlines the HABITS that he teaches his young people. With apologies to Doug, here is our localised version of his excellent idea:

H	Hang Time with God	Listening to God in His Word
		Prayerful Dependence on God
A	Active Ministry	Peer Care
		Peer Evangelism
B	Bible Memorisation	The need to commit to memory
		Some verses to start with (see Appendix)
I	Involvement with Christians	At church - for preaching, worship, celebration
		In your D-Team - for fellowship, equipping, accountability, care
T	Tithing	Learning a lifestyle of generosity
		Financial Stewardship
S	Serving like Jesus	Becoming a servant
		The 'What Would Jesus Do?" challenge
		How to care for fellow believers

Comments:

This step is so vital. If we're going to sow into our young people a heart for ministering to others, we need to help them to make sure that they are walking faithfully with Christ themselves. If we leave this step out, we do them a huge disservice, and place them in a situation where it is easy for the evil one to attack.

iii. How to be a PEER Witness for Jesus

Outcomes of this unit:
- Students will understand their crucial role of being salt and light to their not-yet-saved friends - and be excited by the possibilities.
- Students will be active at their own High School in being PEER witnesses.

Content of this Unit:
- We will teach the crucial ministry of being salt and light to your not-yet-saved friends.
- We will develop boldness and confidence in our Christian students so that they witness from joy, and not from guilt.
- We will teach the 4 step PEER approach to personal witnessing.

P	**Pray**	Learn to pray for not-yet-saved friends Be held accountable in your small group
E	**Encourage**	How to show acts of Christlike love. Developing real relationships with the not-yet saved.
E	**Evangelise**	How to share something of the gospel. The 5 "baby steps" of evangelism (see note below)
R	**Recruit**	How to invite to Crossfire - and other evangelistic events.

Note – The 5 "baby-steps" of evangelism

Students do not have to be able to give a full-blown gospel outline to be evangelistic. We teach then the following 5 "baby steps" to start the on a gospel path:

- Tell your friend you go to Crossfire
- Tell your friend you go to Church
- Tell your friend you're a Christian
- Tell your friend one reason why you're a Christian
- Ask your friend if they're interested in finding out more

Comment:

We want **every** student to reach this level of ministry, where they are intentionally praying for their unsaved friends, looking for ways to show Christ's love to their unsaved friends, being able to say something about their relationship with Jesus to their unsaved friends, and consistently inviting their unsaved friends along to Crossfire and other evangelistic opportunities.

iv. How to Share the Gospel of Jesus

Outcomes of this unit:
- Students will commit to memory a basic outline of the gospel.
- Students will be active at their own High School - informally sharing the gospel in the context of the PEER Witness 4 steps.
- Students will be able to evangelistically counsel those who respond at to God's message.

Content of this unit:
- We teach an adaptation of the "Record Book of Sin" illustration from Evangelism Explosion as a simple way of explaining the gospel. (see Appendix)

  Can I commend "Evangelism Explosion" as a ministry worth pursuing? (further details below) They have excellent material, and I believe their ministry training which we are currently undertaking will revolutionise the life and ministry of many of our students.

b) "No Regrets" Year 12 Ministry

We want to give special support to our year 12 students who are in their final year of high school. This can be a fairly stressful year, and it is easy to "lose" Year 12s into the world of strenuous study and adult night-life! The "No Regrets" Ministry is more of a concept than a programme, but let me show you how it works, and why I list it as a "Sending Out" programme.

"No Regrets" doesn't mean we have lots of extra things for Year 12s to do; it means that we intentionally set out to make Year 12 a very special year for them. Here's the way it works:

i Start of Year Camp

At our week-long discipleship camp for all our high-schoolers at the end of the January holidays, we try to run a "special" section for Year 12s, to build them as a community. Here we launch the "No Regrets" ministry in these terms:

"Picture yourself on your last day at school. Imagine yourself walking out of those school gates for the last time. Wouldn't it be great to reach that day, and know you had "No Regrets" about the way you'd spent your time in the last year of school?"

We challenge students to have "No Regrets" in the following four areas:

- No regrets about the amount of study they have done
- No regrets about how they have handled their family relationships
- No regrets about how their walk with Christ has gone
- No regrets about their personal ministry they have had to their friends at school.

We particularly urge them on the last two issues. Don't let Year 12 be the year that you let your own Christian life slide away. And don't let your last year of school be one where you don't seize the opportunity to bring your friends to Christ.

We remind our students that up to 85% of people who will make a decision for Christ do so before their eighteenth birthday. Year 12 is their last opportunity to work in the "85%' before they move into the "15%" the following year. We really want Year 12 to be a strong year where Christian students reach out to their friends. That is where the emphasis of the "No Regrets" Ministry is. That's why we place it as a "Sending Out" ministry.

We have a badge that we make available for our Year 12s. It simply says "Leaving school with **NO REGRETS**".

ii Easter Beach Camp

Once again, at this camp we run a separate Year 12 section. We try and make it a bit more "luxurious" for them. We strongly urge them to bring their Year 12 friends on this camp, that they might be saved. At this camp we re-assemble the Year 12 community, and we reinforce the ministry of "No Regrets".

iii "No Regrets Study Camp" – July school holidays

This is almost the only "extra" programming we do for "No Regrets". We run a week long non-residential study camp, where as well as providing seven hours supervised study per day, there is a great time of Christian teaching, and warm fellowship and worship together. The bible studies at this camp follow the four-pronged attack of the "No Regrets" ministry.

iv Other incidental times

Of course, the Year 12 community is meeting every week during their "Year Group Time" at Crossfire, and this is a great opportunity to re-inforce the "No Regrets" ministry. I also try to have one or two "Supper after church" invitations so our Year 12s can come over to our place. It's all part of making this final year at school" a little bit special".

v Graduation Service

Round about the time that the Year 12 students leave school, we have a special "Graduation Service" at church. The Year 12s take part, and we have a few of them share with the congregation what it is like for them to leave school – and especially if they have "any regrets".

We then commission these students as they commence their journey into the wider world, and pray for them as a congregation as they are about to face their final exams.

Then we have one final ceremony which highlights their "graduation" from having an active ministry at their school as a student. They each have a clear plastic "baton" on which they have written a message of encouragement. They all go out into the congregation and hand their baton on to a student in a younger year who attends the same school. This is to symbolise that they are "handing on" the responsibility for active student ministry at that school. This reinforces with the students in the younger years how crucial it is for them to have an active Christian witness at school.

Since we have started our "No Regrets" Year 12 Ministry, we have noticed that our own Christian Year 12s seems to stay more committed in their faith. We are certainly doing better at involving new Year 12s in our activities, and seeing some of them won to Christ.

c) Evangelism Explosion Training

We are in our early days of this excellent world-wide ministry which trains everyday Christians to be everyday witnesses. Students work in two's with a trainer, and not only learn an excellent gospel presentation, but are taken into an actual witnessing situation every week where they "Learn by doing".

We are seeing exciting results – even in our early days. And lying ahead of us is the opportunity to take some of our high-schoolers who are trained in Evangelism Explosion and to minister for a couple of weeks in another country. I see this as a strategic missions trip, because we will go and train local youth leaders in how to go back to their churches and equip their own young people to share their faith with their friends. What an excellent way to impact a whole nation for Christ!

2. Train Students to be Leaders

a) The Apprentices Course

Every year, we run a training course aimed at Year 10 and Year 11 Christian Students who want to be trained in leadership. It is called "The Apprentices" intentionally, because it is a very "hands on" approach to training.

The advantages of training students at this age for leadership are:

- We prepare our students for the future when they might be asked to become an adult leader.
- We gain excellent leadership from our students NOW.
- We supplement our stretched leadership resources.
- We raise up a leadership team for our "Year 5 & 6 Discovery Camp" (See Chapter 16).

Here's how it works:

i   Classroom Training

Our year 10 students have one classroom training sessions per term (four per year).   Our Year 11 Students have 2 classroom training sessions per term (eight per year). This is a key time to sow into these young trainee leaders the basics of Christian ministry. The Outline for these training sessions is contained within our overall training schedule in the Appendix.

ii   "Hands On" Training

All Apprentices are involved in helping to lead our younger youth group (Crossfire 68). They work in two teams, and they attend on alternate weeks. They are "apprenticed" alongside one of our adult leadership team, and their ministry is to observe and learn, and get to know the small group of students that they are attached to. We "debrief" from this hands-on training in our classroom time.

iii Studying a book

Our Year 11 Apprentices also study a book on youth ministry each year, and do a book report on each chapter. Which book? This one, of course! ("Hi!" to all the Crossfire Apprentices!)

iv Sharing their Life Story

Our Year 11 Apprentices are taught how to share their " Life Story" of how Jesus has impacted their life (their testimony). They learn to share this in a "public speaking" manner, so that they might present their "testimony" at Crossfire, or some other opportunity for ministry.

v) Camp Leadership

At the end of their year of training, Apprentices become the main leaders at our Year 5 & 6 Discovery Camp. This camp (described in Chapter 16) is an opportunity for these trainee leaders to throw off their "Apprentice" tag, and be leaders for a weekend in their own right.

3. Train Your "Leaders of leaders"

Some special people that can often be left out in the "Sending Out" ministries are your "Leaders of Leaders". That is, as soon as you have more than about 20 leaders, you will need to have them organised so that some leaders take responsibility for other leaders. You need to train your "Leaders of Leaders" a little differently than you train your "Leaders of Students".

At Crossfire, I have 2 staff who work under my direction. They directly oversee our four volunteer Team Leaders. In both junior and senior high we have 2 Team Leaders who are responsible for the ministry in their age group. They oversee the work of our "Year Co-ordinators" who head up the ministry for each specific year group at Crossfire. These year Group Co-ordinators oversee the work of all Crossfire Leaders and D-team coaches for that age group. Nearly all the people listed above are "leaders of leaders".

How do you best help your "Leaders of Leaders"?

a) Give them help in selecting their leaders

Most of our "Leaders of Leaders" will do the initial asking when we are looking for new leaders. I try to give them some guidelines to help them in this task.

Here are the questions my "Leaders of Leaders" should ask when selecting leaders:

i *Their Commitment to Jesus.*

- Are they a Christian?
- Have they been a Christian for a reasonable time? (say... at least 1-2 years)
- Are they growing in strength and maturity as a Christian?
- Are they growing in showing the fruit of the Spirit in their life? (Check out Galatians 5: 22-23)
- If you don't know them well, have you checked them out with someone who does? (e.g. their bible study group leader)

ii. *The Model They Will Set.*

- Would you be happy if students start living their Christian lives like this leader is living his/her Christian life?
- Are there any obvious areas of weakness - or sin - that they don't appear to be making any effort to turn away from?
- Do they have a healthy understanding and open-ness to their own strengths and weaknesses?

iii *Their Qualities As A Leader.*

- Are they growing in showing the qualities that a Christian leader needs to show? (Check out Titus 1: 1-7, 1 Timothy 3: 1-13, 2 Timothy 2: 24-26)
- Are they showing gifts of pastoring and teaching - that is, are they already ministering to those around them?

iv. Their Life In The Body.

•. Have they established themselves as a committed member of THIS congregation over a reasonable period of time (say ... the last year at least) (e.g. church plus a small bible study group)

•. Are they involved with Christian activities for their own learning and growth?

v Their Personal Needs And Relationships

• Have they shown the ability to relate easily to the age group you are considering?   OR   Do they show an open-ness to learning how to relate to a particular age group?

• Are there any personality traits that they are NOT working on which might get in the way of effective ministry?

• Do they have seem to have an excessively strong need to be in a position of ministry?

• Do they show an open-ness and willingness to receive training, advice and help?

•. Do you think they would work comfortably in a team situation - or are they overly independent and tend to "go it alone"?

•. Are they positive, encouraging people?

Remember a "no" to any one question doesn't automatically rule them out (unless it's "Are they a Christian?"), but a "no" indicates "proceed with caution".

b) Train them in encouraging and developing leaders

Here are our guidelines to help our "Leaders of Leaders" strengthen their teams

i. Learn to listen ACTIVELY

It's important to let your leaders know that you have taken in what they've said. Even if you disagree with them, even if you haven't got time right then to deal with it, even if their comment is unimportant to you, let them know that you've heard them.

The simplest way is to

- feed back to them what they've just said. *"It sounds like ..." "You mean ..." "So you want to ..."*
- encourage them that it's okay to feel that way *"That's probably pretty important to you" "Boy - if that was happening to me I think I'd feel ..."*

ii. Learn to care PERSONALLY

Don't just treat your team as "team". Get alongside each person individually. Spend time with them individually. Pray with them. Remember birthdays and special events.

iii Establish high standards of achievable excellence

We're not after "perfection", but we are after "excellence". Expect the best from your leaders. Create a climate where individuals can discover and develop their gifts. Stretch each person to perform at their peak. A challenge to excellence has great power. But keep it realistic!

iv Create an environment where it's okay to fail.

Show how to fail by example. Failure is not as bad as the fear of it. "I'd rather do something great and fail, than to do nothing and succeed". Always treat "failure" as an opportunity for learning.

v Recognise and applaud achievement

Affirm people. Appreciate their efforts and work. Recognise, acknowledge and compliment.

- Commend in public
- Celebrate successes
- Do "little things" to show appreciation
- Compliment in writing
- Be specific in praise

vi. Don't be scared to (gently!) correct

Observe what your leaders are doing, and help them to do better. Be aware where leaders might have "failed", but **don't** realise it, and also where they've "failed" and are feeling very low.

Suggestion - Don't give negative feedback on the same night that it happens!

3 important questions to remember:
a) How do you feel it went?
b) If you did it again, what would you do differently?
c) How can I help you to do it better next time?

vii Train others to take your place

It's important to train leaders on your team to be leaders of leaders. Start giving them extra responsibilities. Share your thoughts and visions with them. Teach them ministry. When your leaders can see the possibilities that lie before them, they will be challenged to perform well.

viii. Build a team.

Your leaders will work the best when they like belonging to your team. So take time to build your team. Spend time together - learn together - achieve together - have fun together.

Share your vision and encourage others to join you in a common vision. Help your team to see what they are achieving, and help them to see that you're achieving it as a TEAM.

ix. Help leaders to feel needed.

There is a big difference between feeling USED and feeling NEEDED. Welcome your leaders' suggestions - use them in preference to your own ideas wherever possible. Don't just do it all yourself - even if your way is better and faster. If you do it all yourself, your ministry will always be limited to what you can achieve. But if you develop others to lead as well - there is no limit to what can be done.

x. Model relationships.

If you want a caring, unified tone in your team, then make sure that that is the way you relate to your co-team leader. If there are tensions there, they will filter down to the whole team. Also, your leaders will see how you play as a "team person" on YOUR team (i.e. with other team leaders). So be an enthusiastic supporter in YOUR team, and that will help your leaders to be enthusiastic for THEIR team.

xi Model godliness

Set a high standard in your own personal Christian integrity. If there are areas where you do not repent - it won't just affect you - it will affect all your leaders - and the kids as well.

xii Model prayer

Set a prayerful tone by your own personal prayer life. Bathe everything in prayer privately, so that it will be natural for you to do it publicly. From the outset, create a climate where your team members will be encouraged to approach everything in prayer.

xiii Inspire!

Your leaders will easily get discouraged. Inspire them and keep their vision big!

4. Train Your Adult Leadership Team

I cannot emphasise how important this area of ministry is. We can't expect high standards from our leaders when we don't train and equip them to reach that level. It is sometimes hard working with volunteers to get them to "come and be trained". But if we're going to sow into our leaders, rather than just "use" them, then this training ministry will really count.

How do we programme this?

We try to do it in a way that doesn't just "add dates" to our leaders' over-full diaries. At the moment we are running some training sessions before or after Crossfire (so it just lengthens the leaders' night out). The other thing we do is we always take breaks for the school holidays (mainly to give our leaders some time-off) and we **always** break one week before school finishes, so on the actual break-up day from school, we have a leaders' celebration night.

The schedule for our "Training of our Leaders" is in the Appendix.

Chapter 16
Programming For Camps

Camping can be a powerful tool to help you in your programming. Many of us have happy memories of the great times we have had on camps, and we know how much the young people at our church look forward to them. But what do they achieve? Why do we have them? What principles can we use so that we programme camps wisely?

1. Plan Your Camp With A Specific Purpose In Mind

Here is the worst way to plan a camp:

> "We need to do something different in our programming"
> "I know – why don't we have a camp?"
> "Excellent idea! Everyone loves camps"
> "When will we go?"
> "How about in two months?"
> "Fantastic! I'll book a camp-site"

And so another youth group camp is underway. But no-one has worked out **why** they are going; no-one knows what the **purpose** of the camp is, and no-one will ever know whether the camp achieved its purposes. Will it be worth running another one next year? Does it need to be different? Who will know?

You don't need a special strategy to plan good camps. Camping is just another programme opportunity to help you achieve your biblical aims. You will ask the same question of a camp that you will ask of any ministry activity.

- Is this the best way to help us "make disciples"?
- Will it help us bring people to Christ?

- Will it help us build up people in Christ?
- Will it help us send people out for Christ?

To have a great camp, work out your purpose **first**. Then determine if a camp is the best way to achieve that purpose. And then plan your camp with your end objective in mind.

At Crossfire we plan for 3 major camps per year.

a) Week-Long Discipleship Camp in Christmas School Holidays

The main aim of this camp is "Building Up". We run this week-long camp in the Christmas school holidays, which is in the middle of summer, and we take our Christian high-schoolers away for a week. The aim of the camp is to build up our disciples so they will be keen to start their school year in active ministry. That is why we place this camp right at the beginning of the year. It is also our "launching pad" for our ministries for the whole year.

We have a heavy emphasis on teaching the bible, and challenging students to a high level of discipleship. We intentionally try to take only the committed students with us. We advertise the camp in these terms "All we do between breakfast and lunch is to study the bible".

We have an awesome time of Christian growth. But there are always a number of interested non –Christians who join with us, so at this camp we provide an opportunity to call them to Christ.

b) Weekend "Beach Camp" just before Easter

This is a major evangelistic push. Our sole aim is to "Bring In" as many students as possible. Both Crossfires (68 and X) each run their own separate camp – right next door to each other. We pick up on the high energy levels during the first term at school, and run this camp to co-incide with the end of this term. By calling many students to follow Christ at this point of the year, this gives us a real focus on "Follow Up" and starting "Discovering Jesus" Courses during Term 2.

We combine for the main teaching times each morning, but apart from that Crossfire 68 and Crossfire X run their own programme. Our Christian students are well geared up for this camp, and many will be praying for their unsaved friends and inviting their unsaved friends along for months before camp. We usually take away a great swag of non-Christian students, and we challenge them to take the step of committing their life to Jesus.

c) Year 5 & 6 Discovery Camp – late November

This is our "Bringing In" Camp at the junior end of town. We advertise this camp through the "Scripture" classes at the six local primary (elementary) schools. We invite these young students to come away for a great weekend where they will discover the difference that Jesus makes to their life. Whilst many of our Year 5s and 6s from our own church come as well, about two thirds of the students who come to this camp will be from outside our church sphere altogether. The aim of this camp is to challenge primary school students to start following Jesus.

We will also organise a "camp reunion" at the beginning of the following year – at the opening night of Crossfire 68. We are intentionally trying to draw students into our ongoing Crossfire ministry, so that they will continue to be exposed to the gospel.

The leaders on this camp are primarily our "Apprentice" trainee-leaders from Year 10 and 11 at High School (explained further in Chapter 15)

d) Other smaller camps

As well as these major camps, we encourage each of our D-teams to have a weekend away together at some stage each year. The main aim of these small "weekends away" is for "Building Up" – especially to develop the supportive relationship within the small group, and to strengthen the bonds of fellowship.

2. Develop The Five Key Relationships Of Camping

What is it that makes camping such a special experience? I believe it has to do with the relationships that form a very special (albeit temporary!)

community. It is the relationships on camp that are the key to programming a successful camp. Here are the Five Key Relationships which will make the ministry of a camp very powerful.

a) Leader / God

One of the most important facets in the successful running of a Christian camp is the individual team member's relationship with God. It is essential that every team member be a committed Christian.

Camps will tend to intensify individual team member's relationship with God. If they are strong in their faith, then camp often makes them a bit stronger. However, if their relationship with God is a bit "shaky", camp often acts as the "final straw" which brings about a crisis in their ongoing life with God.

As well as the individual's relationship with his creator, the team as a whole needs to be committed to God in the task that they are doing. Our life together as leaders - in bible study, prayer and fellowship, is very important.

b) Leader / Leader

What will the campers see when they look at the team as a whole? Will they see a care and concern amongst the various members - a love which reaches out and embraces them as well? Will they see unity among the Christians - working together as a body?

Relationships amongst team members are very important not only for each others' benefit, but for the effect it will have on the campers. Team members need to be sensitive to each other - to care for each other - and to work together as brothers and sisters dedicated to this particular mission. Responsibilities amongst various team members need to be worked out in such a way that people are working together, and not in competition with each other.

The times during camp when the team meets for fellowship are very important. Not just to "let off steam" and iron out problems - but just to be together as Christian brothers and sisters - to pray and join together in serving God.

Just as important are the pre-camp preparation meetings so that the team can grow together, by getting to know each other, and by praying and learning together.

c) Leader / Camper

The key relationship in using Christian camping to confront campers with the claims of Jesus on their life is the relationship that each camper has with his own leader.

A cabin leader or a pastoral group leader enjoys a unique relationship - he is living with the camper for a week, he is "in locos parentis", a teacher, a big brother or sister, a counsellor, a helper, a leader, a shoulder to cry on, a model - all this and much more.

On a 7 day camp, a "cabin leader" will be with the camper for virtually all the time - 168 hours. By comparison, a teacher at a High School, who teaches a child for one 40 minute period every day for a whole year, will be with the child approximately 133 hours. At camp, there are 5 or 6 other campers to share the leader's attention. At school, there are approximately 30 others. The influence that a camp leader can have on a teenager's life is quite considerable - it is a privileged position, and care should be taken that it isn't abused.

Because of the importance of the relationship between the camper and his own leader, the structure of the camp needs to help this relationship to form in a positive way. Other members of staff will of course develop relationships with various campers, and some kids will just "not get on" with their own leader. Relationships with campers are the responsibility of ALL the team, with the key relationship being the camper with his own leader.

d) Camper / Camper

One of the challenges of camp is living as a group. In this highly individualistic society, where isolated people live in isolated houses, living and sharing with others can be a forgotten art! Camp can sometimes be a bit of a "shock to the system" for a camper (and for staff!), for his new "family" has 6 other kids his own age, and the week is spent doing things together, rather than individually.

However, this can be a very useful time, for co-operation becomes very necessary for peaceful survival. Being concerned for each other becomes a more "natural" thing under these conditions, and this can help point towards the outworkings of the gospel. Camps are often a crucial turning point in a camper's social development.

Our "Golden Rule" for happy camps is: "Have fun – but not at anyone else's expense". This enables us all to have a great time, without the constant barrage of practical jokes which always end up with someone being hurt.

e) Camper / God

Our main concern in Christian Camping is the camper's relationship with God. Hopefully, through his leader, each camper will be confronted with the claims of Christ. Everything on the camp should be working towards enabling this to happen - not just in the structured learning times, but in the general way that everything is conducted.

All other relationships on camp are subservient to this one - yet all in some way are helping this vital relationship to grow. The team members' commitment to God, the relationships amongst the various staff, the leader's dealings with his campers, the campers' interaction with each other - should all help and hopefully lead the camper to encountering the living Christ in a way that is very real.

3. Understand the Key Responsibilities of the 'Cabin Leader'

I believe that the absolute key thing to get "right" on a camp is the relationship between a camper and their "own" small group leader. However you plan your camp, arrange your leadership team so that one leader takes personal responsibility for about half a dozen campers. This might be arranged by bible study group, or cabin groups; you might use an existing group arrangement, or make special groups just for camp. You use whatever works best for you.

But make sure that everything you do on the camp helps promote a healthy relationship between each camper and their small group leader. Here is an outline of the responsibilities of the "Cabin Leader"

a) The Camper's Spiritual Growth

This is your main concern. Your most crucial role is to help guide your campers into a closer relationship with Jesus. You are there to help them to become Christians, and to help them to grow as Christians.

i   You will need to give very good attention to the preparation of your bible studies. Looking at them once "the night before" is not good enough.

ii You need to make sure that your studies are pitched "where the campers are at". Be creative and involving! Remember the least effective method of communication is to sit and just talk to kids. Listen for the feedback - and be prepared to change mid-stream. However, don't chuck your message out with your method!

iii Look for "informal" opportunities to get alongside them and continue your ministry with them. If you are sensitive to where each kid is "at", then you can have some valuable ministry this way.

iv The way you live on a camp will speak much more loudly than what you teach. The gospel, after all, is not about words, but about action. Campers will tend to copy and exaggerate your attitudes and actions - so be careful!

v   Be sensitive to kids "becoming" Christians for the wrong reasons. They can easily "make a decision" simply to please you. Take the pressure off!

vi You need to take responsibility for filing in any counselling records etc that reflect the spiritual growth of one of your campers.

b) The Camper's Welfare

You are responsible for your group of campers. Whether it's your cabin group or your bible study group - you are the person who is there in place of their parents.

i Get to know each of your campers - spend some time with each and get to know their individual needs.

ii Be careful about playing favourites. Don't just spend time with the "attractive" kids, or with those you "click" with.

iii Give adequate supervision of all activities - especially those with a higher degree of danger.

iv Take time to explain any particular rules of the camp, and the reasons behind them.

v Make sure you know where each of your group members is at all times. That is, unless another leader has assumed responsibility for them for a short time (e.g. an activity instructor) YOU are responsible for them.

vi You need to make sure that all your kids have arrived at each activity (meals, activities, bible study etc.) Get used to counting! If all your kids aren't there - YOU are responsible for finding them.

vii With sensitivity, encourage good hygiene amongst your campers. Being on camp often means that normal "rules" are forgotten. So, taking into account the age of your campers, encourage daily showering, cleaning hands and teeth, appropriate clothing (including night time!) etc. Female leaders need to be especially aware of girl campers who are having their periods. (especially younger girls!)

viii Keep looking for ways of encouraging each of your kids. Praise their efforts and affirm their strengths. This can have a powerful effect on many kids. Don't ridicule them for their weaknesses!

ix   Be aware of the unsettled emotions that adolescents often have. Whilst you want to form a good relationship, don't form one that is SO close that the camper becomes dependant on you, or is smothered by you (or you by them!) Be especially cautious of forming relationships with campers of the opposite sex. You need to be aware of your own needs and weaknesses, you need to understand that campers can easily misread things, and you need to be very careful that you don't place yourself in situations where you are open to temptation and misinterpretation.

c) Developing Discipline

i   Guide campers in activities which involve work. Hop in with them and set the pace. Don't suddenly absent yourself when the washing up has to start! And don't just do it all yourself! Take your share - and encourage others to take their share too.

ii   Learn to distinguish between "childish irresponsibility" (whoops!) and "wilful defiance" (NO!!) Take action depending on the disruptive effect of the camper's defiance, not on how angry you feel.

iii   Be aware of your own reactions, and your own "triggers" and weaknesses. Make sure you are responding to the camper and his situation, and not just your own hidden agenda. Talk to the kids about what is happening inside of you - don't just talk about what they are doing that's WRONG!

iv   Establish reasonable limits, and give kids freedom within those limits.

v   Stick to your word and mean what you say.

vi   Don't reward inappropriate behaviour.

vii   If action needs to be taken with a camper who has not

responded to your encouragements and has continued with wilful defiance, be very careful about "inventing" a discipline method yourself. This is probably a good time to involve one of the directors or houseparents. Authority from "outside" the group can often have more effect than what you can do yourself. It also enables you to maintain your good relationships with your kids.

viii Sometimes, exclusion from an activity can be appropriate for a camper who is continuing with wilful defiance. This can enable some individual time to be spent with the camper, it can show the camper the consequence of his action, and it can enable your group to accomplish something without distraction. Consult with one of the directors if you think this is the wisest way forward.

ix Encourage your campers to develop self-discipline. Try to give each camper in your group a taste of responsibility during camp - no matter how small it appears to you.

d) The Camp in general

i Be responsible for any equipment that you are using. Teach this sense of responsibility to your kids.

ii Encourage other members of the leadership team, and support them. If you have any differences with other team members, sensitively deal with these privately. Let one of the directors know how things are going.

iii If you can see problems with the camp, or the programme, don't just go around complaining. Talk with one of the directors. Remember - a critical spirit can be very destructive!

iv Stay close to God. Live for him. It is his ministry, and you are a leader under his authority. Do things his way.

v You are there for the kids. Hang in there with them. Don't just socialise with other leaders. Stick with your kids.

vi   Keep the directors informed of how everything is going. Ask about anything you're not sure about. Don't be afraid to call for help!

vii Pray like mad. For each of your kids, for the camp, and that God's will will be accomplished.

4. Principles for Programming

a) Does your programme reflect your purpose and goals?

If your aim is "to bring students to Christ" – does your programme reflect this? Is the "gospel-proclaiming challenge to respond" the centre-piece of your camp? Does everything else on your camp serve this focus? Or does your programme reflect that "endless sports" are the centrepiece of everything you do?

b) Does your programme reflect the age and maturity of your campers?

When we take Years 5 and 6 (10-12 yr olds) on an evangelistic camp, we have one main bible-teaching session in the morning, followed by discussion groups. All this is done before morning tea time. The rest of the morning (and afternoon) is available for recreational activities and free time.

When we take high-schoolers on an evangelistic camp, we have a longer main worship/teaching session in the morning, and after morning tea. we have seminar groups on a variety of topics that the students can choose. After lunch is then available for recreational activities and free time.

When we take our high-schoolers away for a discipleship camp. the whole morning will consist of individual time with God, praise and worship together, preaching, and extended small group interaction on the message. While we usually reserve the afternoon for recreational activities and free time, we may have a second worship and bible teaching session in the evening.

Use your programme to stretch your campers – but use your programme to relax your campers!

c) Does your programme have balance of structured and unstructured time?

Structured times are when everyone is doing the same thing together. The unstructured times are where campers have a genuine choice as to what they do. With younger campers, we tend to allow small amounts of free time (they're often looking for something to do), but as they progress through high school, we give them more and more free time.

Even when you have a range of activities available, students may well just want to "veg out" and sit with their friends. We started offering this as an option on our camps. When students are able to choose between horse-riding, water skiing, water-sliding, abseiling and canoeing, we are surprised by the number of students who choose "home-base" (which basically means, they stay around the "home base" of camp, and "hang" with their friends).

If you allow for too much free time, then students will become bored and restless, perhaps destructive (and will never get to sleep at night). If you allow too little free time, students will be over-stressed and irritable (and they will "wear out" too quickly). Be prepared to "go with the flow" and change your plans if necessary.

I went on a camp once (as an adult) where we had 5 "lectures" a day for 3 days – with no free time! Aarrgghh! Despite the good things on that camp, I was sure glad when it finished!

5. Dangers To Avoid

Camping provides so many great opportunities for ministry – and we find that they are a particular help in our "bringing in" ministry. Many many Christian students at Crossfire will attest to the fact that their real commitment to follow Jesus was made on a camp.

But there are three dangers we need to be aware of:

a) Overtiredness

Especially with a week-long camp, the dangers of over-tiredness are high. Some unfortunate results of over-tiredness are:

- Students will become more accident-prone.
- Students' emotions will be very "raw" - which can result in a lot of crying ... which can result in ...
- Students can make a decision to "follow Jesus" for purely emotional reasons.

We need to be people of integrity when we take students away on camp. By allowing them to become over-tired, we do not care for them in a Christlike way.

> " ... we were gentle among you, like a mother caring for her little children."
> **1 Thessalonians 2:7**

If they make a response on camp – based on their over-tiredness – or a rush of emotion – it will not be "fruit that will last".

b) Not preparing students for "re-entry" into the real world

We need to understand that camp is not the way the real world is. Maybe it is a little taste of heaven, but it is not the normal world that God has called us to minister in. We do students a dis-service if we do not prepare them for re-entry to the "real world".

The "post-camp blues" can be a real problem for teenagers, if all their hopes and expectations have been centred on their one-week experience. We need to enjoy the privileges of being away on a Christian community, but not abuse that privilege by encouraging students to make responses based on the wonderful feeling of being on camp. Responses that are "just for camp" will not produce "fruit that will last".

c) Encouraging Camp Groupies

I can remember asking a Christian student one week at church "How's your Christian life going?" "Not too good at the moment" he answered me

"But it will get better when I go to my next Christian camp in the holidays"

Hmmm.

We need to work hard on our camps so that students do not see them as their "Saviours". Camps are a break from a regular routine to enable us to focus on the things of God more clearly. If we want to produce "fruit that will last", we must work hard at developing strong disciples who will survive and prosper in a world that is full of difficulties – and not just produce disciples who can be strong while they're in the "hot-house" of a camp.

Chapter 17
2 Valuable Servants of Programming

I want to focus on two valuable servants of youth programming which have enormous potential to be a huge help to your ministry of making disciples. But you need to be cautious with these servants – they have the potential to take over and become your masters! And as your masters they will take you away from producing "fruit that will last". But used wisely, these two things will be a huge blessing as you build a ministry that really produces "fruit that will last".

1. The 'Altar Call'

This is kind of an unfortunate name - but I use it because most youth leaders will know what I am talking about. When I say "altar call" I am speaking about the method by which you publicly call students to make a commitment to Christ. When it comes down to programming, "how" you do this needs to be thought through carefully.

a) Make sure the gospel has been proclaimed

If you are asking people to respond, make sure they have a clear message of the gospel on which to base their decision. Clarity in your preaching will avoid muddiness in your followup!

b) Work out what method you will use

If you are going to publicly challenge students to become Christians, then you need to have thought through "how" you will get them to make a response. There are many alternatives.

i "Come out the front and stand publicly before us"

This is an excellent method when you have a large crowd. I like it because:

- It is immediate – students are challenged to do something NOW.
- It is public – it challenges students to have a real and public commitment to Christ.
- It encourages the Christians – because they can see their friends walking forward – and they can pray for them while they do it (or even go out with them to support them).
- It makes follow up immediate - those who will follow up meet the enquirers out the front, and can chat with them straightaway.

It gives you the opportunity to be specific as to the people you are inviting to respond. Many years ago I was privileged to be one of the Advisers at the Evangelistic Rallies held by Leighton Ford – a gifted evangelist of high integrity. By listening to Leighton make an appeal night after night at the Wayville Showgrounds in Adelaide, I learned there are 3 categories of enquirers you are inviting to respond when you ask people to "come forward" and make a public commitment to Jesus.

- Those who want to make a first-time commitment to follow Jesus – come out and make that commitment.
- Those who are not sure if they've made a real commitment already – come out and make sure.
- Those who have made a commitment before, but you know you have wandered a long way from Jesus – then come out if you want to come back.

If you're using this method, you need to …

- Think through carefully **how** you will invite people to respond.
- Be prepared to invite further enquirers to join you – even as you're assembling the crowd at the front, it is always good to ask if any more want to join you.
- Make sure you have leaders available to talk with those who respond.

- Ensure that you have follow up material available that night for those who need them.
- Have somewhere where you can talk with the enquirers separate from the rest of the crowd.
- Allow time in your programme for the enquirers to be counselled.

Warning: The "Come out the front and stand publicly before us" method of response seems to be the **most** open to abuse. Be careful! (see below!)

ii "Stay behind when everyone leaves"

This is a lower-key alternative to the above, and may be more suitable when you have a smaller crowd, or when it would not be appropriate to have people come forward in front of everyone.

To do this effectively, use similar methods to above, but at the end, you invite the crowd to leave the building, and as they leave, genuine enquirers can meet with you and other leaders out the front. If appropriate, you can then take the enquirers to a more suitable setting for ongoing help.

iii "Everyone fill in a response card"

This can be useful when it is more appropriate **not** to commence initial follow up on the same night. If you have a response card, and you invite everyone to fill it in, this probably makes it easier for the genuine enquirers to be a little more anonymous.

If you use this method, you need to be aware that sometimes you will get some "fake" cards returned, where students have used an imaginary name and address, or filled in the name of their **friend** on their own card!

Also, be careful that you don't make the responses so general that **everybody** fills in the response box! Many years ago, our church had a mission where over two weeks we had many evangelistic activities, and at every one of these, everyone was asked to fill in a response form. Unfortunately, the response card was worded a little bit vaguely, and the response to indicate you wanted to become a Christian was "I prayed the prayer with the preacher". We discovered that people who had been Christians for over 10 years were filling it in – not because they wanted to make some radical difference to their walk with Christ, but simply because they had prayed when the preacher invited them to.

If your response options are too vague, you will be overwhelmed with "unnecessary" responses , which will make your follow up very difficult.

iv "Eyes closed, hands up"

This method asks everyone to close their eyes, and put their hands up if they want to respond. While this might be a useful "first step" (that is, at the end, you ask everyone who put their hand up to come out the front and talk with you), by itself, I don't think the "Eyes closed, hands up" method works well.

We had a guest speaker who used this method once at Crossfire, and he excitedly told us at the end of his talk that 8 students had responded by putting their hands up. But because he was the only person who saw them, and he didn't know who anyone was, we were unable to follow any one up!

c) **Determine you will use that method with integrity**

i   Strike while the iron is hot

Whatever method you use, make sure you are ready to help people take that next step at the time that they indicate they would like to do something.

If you use the "Fill in the response card" method, then you need a team of people to process those card and make contact with those people **within 48 hours.** If you do not make quick contact, you may well lose the momentum of helping them take that next step.

If you use the "Stay behind when everyone leaves" method, you need to finish your meeting very shortly after the message. I was speaking at a combined youth outreach night where after I spoke evangelistically, the compere asked people to stay behind at the end and talk if they wanted to enquire further. But then the band played another half a dozen numbers, and the crowd went back to "frantic moshing", so by the time the programme had ended, any impetus we had to follow up those who were responding had been lost.

Jesus said. "And this is the will of him who sent me, that I shall lose none of all that he has given me, but raise them up at the last day". **John 6:39**

That is the key verse for our follow up. That we will lose none of those whom the father has called. So – strike while the iron is hot.

ii Don't manipulate

The "Come out the front and stand publicly before us" method seems to be the one most open to abuse. Here are some guidelines we use so that this becomes an opportunity for genuine responses, rather than the manipulation of a vulnerable crowd.

- Don't use this method "every week". If you are not careful, you will inadvertently "programme" your teenagers to make a "response" every time there is a message. I believe many "altar calls" are done to help the preacher deal with his own insecurity. Some preachers don't believe they have "done well" unless they can get ever increasing percentage of the audience to get out of their seat and come forward.

- Don't appeal endlessly on the one night. If no-one is responding, that's okay. If only a small number respond, that's okay. Don't cajole people into a response by your constant bleating!

- Be careful in your use of music. Music is to reinforce the message, not to manipulate a response.

- Be specific about the response you are asking for. It is more helpful to get a smaller response from asking for "people who are making a first-time commitment to follow Jesus" than to get virtually everyone out of their seat with "come forward if you want to be stronger for Jesus".

The "altar call" can be an excellent servant in that it brings to a head the message that has been proclaimed, and challenges people for a definite response. But let's be careful with it. Let's make sure that we can say along with the apostle Paul ...

> " .. we have renounced secret and shameful ways; we do not use deception, nor do we distort the word of God. On the contrary, by setting forth the truth plainly we commend ourselves to every man's conscience in the sight of God."
> **2 Corinthians 4:2**

2. Music

Oh – I love music! I love listening to music, and I love playing music. I am indeed a "closet musician", and although I am not involved publicly in music very much, it always remains a private passion for me. Some of my greatest moments of worship and fellowship have been with the congregation of God's people in joyful song. What a picture of the perfect creation which awaits those of us who are in Christ Jesus!

a) Why do we use music in youth ministry?

Go to any church. Go to any youth ministry. Music and singing are central. Most people enjoy it. Many absolutely love it! But let's ask the question "Why do we have it?"

I guess the answer is a biblical one. If you scan the pages of the Old Testament there is reference after reference to God's people singing when they gathered together. Those gatherings at the temple must have been full of music and singing! There are instructions to musicians - there are encouragements to singers - indeed there is a whole song book called "The Psalms" – and some psalms even include the name of the tune that was to be used! There is no doubting the place of music life of God's Old Testament people when they gathered around him.

When we look forward to the church that is gathered in heaven, it is obvious that singing and music are part of that heavenly gathering. Revelation 5:9, 5:12, 14:3, 15;3 clearly show us that the church of heaven is a singing church - praising God through music and song.

When we look at the New Testament church, music is still there. We see that the apostles sing a hymn or two (in the garden – Matthew 26:30 – when they're trapped in prison – Acts 16:25). Individual believers are urged to sing (1 Corinthians 14;11, James 5:13), and the Old Testament exhortations to sing are reinforced in Romans 15: 9-11.

Here are the key references to **congregational** singing:

I Corinthians 14:26

What then shall we say, brothers? When you come together, everyone has a hymn, or a word of instruction, a revelation, a tongue or an interpretation. All of these must be done for the strengthening of the church.

This seems to assume that Christians will sing when they come together, and Paul urges them to make sure that it is done "for the strengthening of the church"

Ephesians 5:19-20

Speak to one another with psalms, hymns and spiritual songs. Sing and make music in your heart to the Lord, always giving thanks to God the Father for everything, in the name of our Lord Jesus Christ.

Colossians 3:16-17

Let the word of Christ dwell in you richly as you teach and admonish one another with all wisdom, and as you sing psalms, hymns and spiritual songs with gratitude in your hearts to God. And whatever you do, whether in word or deed, do it all in the name of the Lord Jesus, giving thanks to God the Father through him.

These two parallel passages show us that music and song is where Christians minister to each other, and should be done in a spirit of thanks to God.

There's enough information in the New Testament to indicate that music and singing is a good activity that we should be involved in.

But, to get back to my original question – "Why do we have music and singing in youth ministries around the world?", my suspicion is that the real reason might have very little to do with the New Testament material.

Don't misunderstand me – there's nothing wrong with music and singing as part of what Christians do when they come together. It is a good biblical activity encouraged by the Scriptures.

But here is my worry:

The dominance of music in so many youth ministries might have little to do with the biblical material, and more to do with the fact that ..

- Music is so enjoyable (the entertainment value is high)
- We are fascinated by the superb giftedness of many musicians (and the awesome sound systems that accompany them!) (The Corinthian problem of being fascinated by gifts?)

Hey – let's have the best music we can, and let's sing with all our hearts. Let's follow the biblical encouragement to minister to each other through song – and to give thanks and praise to God through song. I praise God for the faithful Music Directors and musicians at my own church! They do an awesome job!

But let's keep it in perspective. Music is a helpful servant in our biblical task of making disciples. But it is not our master. We do not arrange everything else around the music. It is a helpful servant in the ministry of "making disciples". But it is not the central ministry that actually makes disciples!

If we're not careful, we'll start thinking that "worship" only means singing songs!!

b) They key for keeping your musicians "disciple focussed"

I want to encourage everyone of our young disciples to discover their gifts and serve the body in ministry. This will include our musicians and singers using those abilities to encourage the rest of us to praise God and celebrate our unity.

But if we're going to be faithful pastors to our young musicians, we need to take extra care. There are many dangers for young Christians who are good musicians or singers.

i   "Spotlight" ministries can lead to pride

For better or worse, musicians are placed in the spotlight. They are often out the front. The spotlight is indeed upon them. People's attention is focussed on them. The ministry they perform is very public. Even though they are not in "leadership" as such, young musicians can be treated like they are "leaders". Even though 1 Tim 3:6 is written about "overseers" in the congregation, I believe the principle still applies to those who are in "spotlight ministries" – if you place a young Christians there, the devil might move in and puff them up with pride.

"He must not be a recent convert, or he may become conceited and fall under the same judgment as the devil."
1 Timothy 3:6

ii   Musicians must develop real servanthood

All ministries must develop real servanthood, but we need to work extra hard to help our musicians in this area. Why? Simple - because we are asking young disciples to use music in the **opposite** way from how it is used the rest of the time. Music is a generally a performance talent. Most musicians like to play to an audience. Nearly every musician likes to hear the applause and the accolade of their hearers. Nothing wrong with that. I love to play for an audience myself!

But because music and singing have this inherent "performance" factor which is central to the art, we need to work harder with our young musicians to help them see themselves as servants.

We must help them to develop the attitude of Christ Jesus himself.

"Your attitude should be the same as that of Christ Jesus: Who, being in very nature God, did not consider equality with God something to be grasped, but made himself nothing, taking the very nature of a servant, ...".
Philippians 2:5-7

When youth music sees itself as a servant of the youth ministry, and congregational music sees itself as a servant of the congregation, it is a valuable and faithful servant. But if we don't watch it carefully, it will lose its servant edge, and become the master of all that we do.

Developing servant hearts has certainly been a bit of a problem for us in our youth ministry over the past few years. It all centred around "Who from the vocal group will be invited to become one of the three solo singers who get their own microphone?"

Despite our best efforts, whoever we selected – it still seemed to result in a problem. Sometimes it was a problem of pride for the person who was chosen. Sometimes it was a problem of envy for those not chosen. We urged our students to develop servant hearts, but in the end it still remained as a problem, So for the time being, we have no solo singers with their own mike. We mike the whole vocal group and focus on the sound they produce as a united body.

iii Don't let music ministries take students away from disciple-making ministries

We love having our students involved in the creative arts ministries. But these ministries can be very time demanding – as rehearsals need to be undertaken to produce a quality outcome. We try to keep our young musicians disciple focussed by ensuring that creative arts ministries do not take them away from their central role as a disciple-maker.

We don't want them to be missing from their Discipleship Team because of rehearsal demands. We don't want them so tied up with music ministry that they no longer are able to have a ministry to their unsaved friends. We want them to focus on the "every member" ministries of Peer Care and Peer Witnessing, before they get involved in a "specialist" ministry like music or dance. We want them to discover their "disciple-making" gifts, as well as their more obvious musical talent. We want to equip them for "everyday ministry" in this world first, and then to develop their specialist role in music.

c) Why we don't sing at Crossfire

We don't use congregational music at Crossfire. We sometimes use "presentation" music – where a performer performs a song for the audience that helps them to think about the issues that we are dealing with that night. But we don't use music where we invite the audience to sing.

Why not? Simply because we are aiming Crossfire at the "first-timer". We try to do things that would make it easy for the "first-timer" to feel very much "at home". By the time we get to the preacher standing up to deliver a message, we want everything to be as "user-friendly" as possible.

Australians don't indulge in that much community singing (except when they're drunk!) For the average student in our region, "community singing" would not be a normal part of his everyday life. So we don't do it at Crossfire.

This doesn't mean that you shouldn't do it at your evangelistic ministry. But you should ask the questions "Why are we singing? Is this the best way to help us achieve our objectives?"

I simply want to point out that it is **possible** to have an evangelistic ministry without having singing (or even a band) to "warm up the crowd". I have a feeling that Jesus managed to evangelise well without a large music ministry!

SECTION 6

How to Last In A Ministry That Will Grow

Chapter 18
Staying Fresh For The Long Haul

How long does the average volunteer youth leader stay in youth ministry? How long does the average full-time youth pastor stay in youth ministry? Depending on which surveys you read, the answer is anything from only12 to 36 months! Not long at all, really.

Most people don't stay long enough in youth ministry to ever get good at it.

I believe this is one of the evil one's cleverest attacks. He knows how strategic youth ministry is. He know the battle that is going on to gain the allegiance of a young heart and mind. He knows that if he can get a person through to adulthood without a commitment to Christ taking place, that his chances of that commitment ever taking place are greatly diminished.

So it's all rather clever. The best way for the devil to deal with enthusiastic young youth leaders is to get them disenchanted quickly enough so that they will leave before they ever start to have a real impact. I see it so often. Someone fresh and young comes into youth ministry with idealistic aims, and often within two years they are disillusioned, and looking for something "a little bit easier".

Even the youth pastor – who has done three years at Bible College, sometimes never even lasts that long in one church.

I've been at this for over twenty one years now. I've seen many youth leaders come and go. And yet I believe I am as passionate now for youth ministry as I ever was.

So what are the keys for "lasting" in youth ministry so that you have a harvest that gets more and more bountiful as you go?

Here is what God has taught me over the past twenty one years.

1. Don't Believe You're Superman

You cannot deal with all the problems of every young person. You do not have the answers to every situation. If you believe that you do, you will burn out really quickly.

2. Learn to withdraw to be with God.

Even Jesus often took time out from his ministry to the crowds to be alone. Alone with his Father. Alone in prayer. Sometimes alone with his disciples. But it was a feature of his ministry. Look up your online bible and do a search for the word "withdrew" in the gospels, and see for yourself how important this was to Jesus.

(See Matthew 12:15, 14:13, Mark 3:7, Luke 5:16, 9:10, John 6:15)

3. Remember what your job is.

Don't try and take over God's job. He is quite able to do it himself. Our job as "pastors" is to be faithful in bringing his message to bear in the lives of others. It is God's job to cause change in their heart. He brings people to himself. He brings growth in the life of the believer. If you feel you are responsible for every person's response, you will not last long.

> *"I planted the seed, Apollos watered it, but God made it grow."*
> *1 Corinthians 3:6*

4. Don't work harder than God

God rested one day in seven. Go ye and do likewise! Apart for emergencies, protect your "day off" from ministry so you have a chance to unwind. Put the answering machine on if you have to. Get away from the house. Lead a balanced life.

5. Remember, ministry comes from the overflow of your heart.

If you do not have a heart of integrity, you will never have a ministry of integrity. The ministry that you have - the words that you speak - in the end can only come from a heart that is right with God.

"Out of the overflow of the heart, the mouth speaks"
Matthew 12:34

So guard your heart. Immerse yourself in God. Spend time with him. Listen to him. Talk with him. Worship him. Repent for him.

6. Raise up other leaders to have all the fun!

You probably wanted to get into youth ministry because you wanted to **do** youth ministry. That is, you wanted to do it **yourself**. It's fun to hang out with kids, and be a counsellor to kids, and bounce off the energy of kids.

But if you keep doing that year after year, it will probably drag you down. And if you're doing all the same things now that you did five years ago in youth ministry, then it sounds like your ministry probably isn't expanding. Anything which is stagnant is hard to stick at.

One way to stay fresh is to raise up others to do the things that you've been practising for a while. Then you get the joy of helping someone else start out in leadership. Then your own ministry will expand because rather than always being "hands on", you now start to develop younger leaders into those ministries.

7. Look for the encouragements in the lives of your kids

Those pesky Year 8s that are sending you around the twist - will you stay long enough to enjoy their maturity in Year 11? When you are determined to stay for the long haul, you get to see the fruit of your ministry. The difficulty with youth ministry is that not much of the fruit is immediate. Sometimes it takes years to develop. And most youth leaders leave before they get to see it reach fruition!

I love watching our young people grow and develop. I am thrilled when I sit with my Year 10s and remember how much they've matured since they were bratty Year 7s. I am so encouraged when I see one of our high-schoolers grow in Christlikeness. Look carefully at your young people, and develop "Christlike" eyes – so that you see the work of God in their life.

Celebrate every small encouragement in every student– and hang around to watch it develop and grow!

8. Get your students into active ministry.

Very little gives me a bigger thrill than seeing one of our students active in ministry. It is so good when you know they have been praying for their friend to be saved, and then they have the privilege of bringing them to Christ!

Take students with you when you minister. If you're helping someone come to Christ, involve one of your Christian students with you so they learn ministry with you.

Youth leaders who develop their students into active youth ministry usually last longer.

9. Deepen your family relationships

For all of us, the time we put in with our mum and dad – and our brothers and sisters – really matters. This is particularly true for the single youth leader. Sure - no family is perfect. Every family has problems. But your family is for life – and as far as it is possible, try and keep the relationships healthy. It is great to have family members able to stand by you when things go wrong,

For those of you who are married – especially if you get married while you are already in youth ministry - be prepared to invest large amounts of time into your spouse. This probably means putting less time into the kids at church. You will be less available for spontaneous outings and super-late nights.

But don't resent this. The time you sow into your spouse will pay rich dividends. You will be developed and shaped by your partner, and even though you will have less time available for your youth, you will minister to them as a much more "whole" person.

I didn't realise all this when I got married. It took years for me to learn this. (My wife would probably say I still haven't learned it!) But God is changing me. Hang in there with me, honey!

When you have your own children, you need to make another adjustment. **You will have less time available for youth ministry**. But again, being a "dad" or "mum" will bring out qualities in your character that you did not know you possessed. So with less time, you will have just as great an impact.

When you have a spouse – and children, you just need to learn to be around at home a lot. I have 3 nights where I am committed to be out each week. Every Sunday Night I am at church (with my wife and 2 kids). Every Friday Night I am at Crossfire (with my 2 kids). Every Thursday Night I coach soccer (with my son). I try really hard to be "home" most other nights. Just around. Around if I'm needed. Around for my family to talk with. Just around. The only way I can do this is to consistently say "no" to the myriad of people who are demanding my time at night. Sure – emergencies still happen. Sometimes it doesn't work very well. But I make it a priority to be home whenever I can.

For the past 6 years I have coached my son's soccer team. This is a 10 hour per week commitment. It means I am not available for most Saturday ministries between April and September. It means sometimes we need to play a game on Sunday. But I believe this is a commitment worth making, and for those of you with children, I encourage it strongly.

10. Find others to complement your strengths and weaknesses

Know what you're good at, and what you're not good at. And try and team with people who balance out your strengths and weaknesses. If you really can't get a handle on day by day administration, work in close partnership with someone who can, so you don't have to carry the whole load. If you find it hard to be creative, work with someone who can balance this.

11. Have your own supportive friends

This is an area I am not that good at. I am wired more as an "introvert", so I'm often feeling a bit "peopled out" at the end of a day. But it is important to have your own friends – of your own age, and not always hang out with younger people.

12. Find a mentor

Is there someone who is an older and wiser Christian that you can make yourself accountable to? Someone who will listen and understand, but also someone who help keep you on track. Try and make this someone from outside your own church.

Is there a fellow youth pastor from another church that you can simply hang out with and be refreshed? Youth ministry can be a lonely job. Share your life with someone who can refresh you.

13. Don't forget to have fun.

C'mon – don't take yourself so seriously. Work out what you really enjoy. Unwind a little and let your hair down. This world is here for you to enjoy in a way that brings honour to Christ.

14. As you grow older, understand the different stages of youth ministry.

As you get older, your role will change. Be aware of these changes. If you don't make the changes, you will not last long.

Stage 1 – The "One of the Gang" Stage

This is where you are a young youth leader of (say) 18 and the kids you lead are about 16. There's only a few years difference between you. You know their culture well because you live in their culture. You like the same music as the kids; you wear the same clothes; you do the same things.

You will often have instant acceptance by kids and you will have easy accessibility to everything they do. You will identify with kids strongly and passionately argue their causes for them. But you might not be able to lead them very far, because your life experience will be not much more developed than theirs. You might need the counsel of some older people to make sure your decisions are wise. You probably won't have a deep biblical perspective on what you do, and you may need others to "pull you into line" sometimes.

Stage 2 – The "Big Brother or Sister" Stage

This is where you're about 5 or 6 years older than the kids. Too old to be "one of their friends", but about the right age to be a "big brother" or "big sister".

The students will now look up to you more than in the previous stage, and you knowingly or unknowingly will start to be a role model. You will still be close enough to the kids' culture to understand it well, but you may listen to a different radio station and be a little less in touch with the current "fad". You will probably have more money and more access to transport than the kids, and so they will start to depend on you more.

You are still ministering to kids from within their same culture, but you might find you are a little more annoyed by them than in the 1st stage. Parents may still look at you a bit suspiciously, and may be reticent to trust their teenagers to you. But once you have won their trust, they will value you as a role model.

Stage 3 – The "Uncle or Aunty" Stage

You are now in your mid twenties to mid thirties. This is the first of the "longer stages" (that is, it lasts for at least ten years). You are now too old to be a "big brother or sister" and too young to be the same age as the kids' mum and dad. So you now take the role of a kindly uncle or aunt.

This is a dangerous stage. So many youth leaders "drop out" when they hit this stage. **Because this is the first stage when you start ministering to kids from outside your culture.**

Here is what I mean. In the "Uncle or Aunty" stage, you no longer listen to the same music as the teens. In fact, you probably don't even know the name of most of their songs. And their music is nowhere near as good as the music you had in your teens! You now watch different movies, wear different clothes, have different mannerism and go to different places. Your own family situation is often changing, either by simply moving out of home, or perhaps by marrying. If you are not marrying, you might be asking deep questions about yourself and what your future holds.

Because you are now no longer a part of youth culture, many youth leaders feel at this stage that they have "lost it". You no longer understand kids, and you feel "locked out" of their culture.

And many of these things are true! **But that doesn't mean you have to give up!** It simply means that youth ministry for you is now a **"cross-cultural"** ministry. That is, you can now reach and penetrate a culture as someone who belongs to another culture. You now live on the planet "adult-land". You are only a visitor to the planet "youth-land". Whether you are a **welcome** visitor depends on how well you acclimatise to doing cross-cultural work.

If you can make this transition – you are set for a long and fruitful youth ministry. I haven't been anywhere **near** youth culture for many a long year. I don't know the intimate details of youth culture – I don't know what their music is – I certainly don't particularly **like** their music. (give me classic rock any day!) I am a stranger from another planet.

But here's the good news. To do cross-cultural ministry, you don't have to join the culture you are ministering to., You don't have to pretend to belong. **You don't have to like it or understand it. You just simply need to understand that their culture exists, and that your teenagers live in it.**

Teenagers will accept any adult – no matter what planet you come from – if you are prepared to give them time. Time. That's all they want. And when you show that you are prepared to spend time with them – it is the most valuable of commodities and it speaks powerfully about who you are and what you represent.

Don't pretend you belong to their culture, but simply accept that they are locked in their culture and see everything in terms of their culture. You need to know a little about their culture – and the best way to do this is simply to listen. Hang out with a bunch of teenagers and listen for about half an hour and you will know enough about their culture to know where the entry points for ministry are.

This is a fantastic stage of youth ministry. Accept that it is now "cross cultural". Don't quit because it is so different, but enjoy it. Youth ministry gets **easier** every year I get older!

iv – The "Parent" Stage

This lasts from your mid thirties to your mid fifties. Quite frankly, you are now close in age to the that of the teenagers' own parents. (I have been entrenched in this stage for years!) You may well have teenagers of your own which will bring you a whole new perspective of how youth ministry looks from a parent's viewpoint!

If you managed to make the cultural adjustment in the "uncle or aunty" stage, then the "parents" stage is a breeze! I love it! I am now absolutely from another planet from my teenagers. I get balder and balder and I have a crook back with sciatica. All the kids know I am somehow locked in a time warp from the sixties, but this has got to be the best stage from which to minister to young people (I haven't got to Stage 5 yet!)

In Stage 4 you can minister with wisdom. I find far more teenagers will come and cry with me now than when I was a younger youth pastor. They will now ask really deep questions about their life, and be accepting of my answers. Their parents too will also turn to oldies like me for wisdom about bringing up their kids. Younger youth leaders look for wisdom as they tread the path that I trod over twenty years ago.

It's taken me this long to actually figure out where I am going in youth ministry. When I look back at my days when I was in my mid twenties – I'm amazed God stuck with me. I had all the enthusiasm in the world, but I had no idea of what I was doing! I would never want to go back there!

Can I plead with you – hang on until at least Stage 4 of youth ministry and you will reap so many rewards! (so will the teenagers!) (so will the kingdom!)

v   Stage 5 – The "Grandparent" Stage

I haven't got to this one yet, so all this is prophetic. This stage lasts from about mid fifties until death. You are now much older than the teenagers' parents – and you fit better into the "grandparent" mould.

I'll write more about this stage when I get there, but I suspect there is a huge affinity between teenagers and grandparent figures.

You know the difference between a parent and a grandparent? Grandparents have time. Oodles of it.

Roll on them advancin' years!

If you understand how each stage is different - if you understand the pluses and minuses of each stage – then you'll be better equipped for a long and fruitful ministry with those wonderful people called teenagers.

15. Keep your vision big

The one thing that helps me most to keep going in the long haul – is to keep my vision as big as God's. I am not here to run youth groups – I am here to help raise an army of disciples who will impact the nations of this world for Christ. I am here to sow into the lives of young people so that they might be the church leaders and the church planters in the coming decades.

I get to work with labourers who are called "at the beginning of the day" – and have a whole lifetime of active service ahead of them!

Keep your vision big. Keep your heart big. And you'll keep your ministry big. And long!

Hang in there! Thanks for taking this journey with me

And please buy my next book!

Appendix 1 - Our Vision

1. Why does Crossfire exist?

We exist to give huge honour to our awesome God

2. What does God want us to achieve

We will impact the world for Christ by empowering students to be passionate disciples of Christ

3. How do we make disciples?

By bringing our friends to Christ; by building each other up in Christ; and by sending us out for Christ.

Appendix 2 – Crossfire Strategy

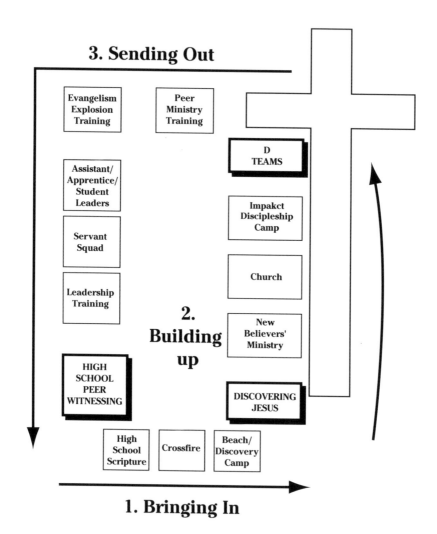

Appendix 3 – Sample Camp Programme

FRIDAY

am	Advance party leaves to set up during Friday
6.00	Yr 789 Rego
6.15	Yr 789 Load
6.30	Yr 789 Depart
6.45	Yr 10-12 Rego
7.00	Yr 10-12 Load
7.15	Yr 10-12 Depart
8.30	Yr 789 Arrive
9.15	Yr 10-12 Arrive
	Evening Programme (separate)
	Official Welcome
	Vision for weekend
	Room allocation
10.00ish	Supper (separate)
10.30ish	Bed

SUNDAY

7.15	Rise
7.30	Orderlies
8.00	Breakfast (separate)
8.45	Clean Up, Band rehearsal
9.00	Free Time
	Snack Shack/Bookstore
9.30	"Rage and Praise" (together)
10.00	Sermon 2
10.30	Challenge to Respond
10.45	Counselling / Morning Tea
11.00	Casual Activities
12.00	Orderlies
12.30	Lunch (together)
1.15	Cleanup
2.15	Final Get together
2.45	Pack everything
3.00	Depart
5.00	St. Paul's

SATURDAY

7.15	Rise
7.30	Orderlies
8.00	Breakfast (separate)
8.45	Clean Up
	Band rehearsal
9.00	Free Time
9.30	"Rage and Praise" (together)
10.00	Sermon 1
10.30	Morning Tea/
	Snack Shack/Bookstore
11.00	Seminars
12.00	Break / orderlies
12.30	Lunch (together)
1.15	Cleanup
1.30	Afternoon activities Snack Shack/Bookstore
4.30	Leaders gathering for prayer (for those who are on site)
5.15	Orderlies
5.45	Tea (separate?)
6.45	Cleanup
7.30	Evening Activities (together)
10.00	Supper (together) Bookstore
10.30	Bed (separate)

Appendix 4 – Sample Bible Teaching at Crossfire

		Passage	Topic	Issues
Apr 23	1	John 8: 21-30	Will I really make it?	• "You will die in your sins. You cannot go where I am going" • When Jesus is lifted up on the Cross, people will know that he is the "I am" • Many believed
Apr 30	2	John 8: 31-47	Am I really free?	• Jesus' disciples will know the truth and the truth will set them free • Free from what? Being a slave to sin. • You're no longer a slave but a son • If the Son sets you free - you're really free! • Those who really have God as their Father will love Jesus • Otherwise, your father is the devil - and you will want to follow your father's desires
May 7	3	John 8: 48-59	Is Jesus really God?	• Jesus seeks to honour the father • If you obey Jesus you will never die • Jesus knows the Father, and obeys his word • "Before Abraham was - I am" • They picked up stones to throw at him
May 14	4	John 9	How can I be so blind? (Healing the Blind man)	• Jesus heals the blind man • The Pharisees are upset with Jesus • "One thing I do know. I was blind, but now I can see" • Jesus can heal your "spiritual" blindness

		Passage	Topic	Issues
May 21	5	John 10: 1-21	Will Jesus protect me? (The Good Shepherd)	• Jesus is the good shepherd who lays down his life for his sheep • he is not a "hired hand" who will run away • Jesus wants to give "life to the max"
May 28	6	John 10: 22-42	Will Jesus hang on to me? (Safe in the Father's Hand)	• When you are saved, you are safe in God's hand • No-one can snatch you away
June 4	7	John 11: 1-44	What happens when I die? (Lazarus) -	• Jesus weeps for his friend Lazarus • "I am the resurrection and the life" • "Lazarus – come out!"
June 11	8	John 11: 45-57	Why did Jesus have to die?	• The chief priests are jealous of Jesus and his popularity • "One man should die for the people" • "From that day on they plotted to take his life"
June 18	9	John 12: 1-10	What should I offer to Jesus? (Anointing at Bethany)	• Mary offered something hugely valuable to her • Jesus accepts this as anointing for his burial
June 25	10	John 12: 12-19\	How should I worship Jesus? (Jesus' triumphal entry)	• Jesus enters Jerusalem – as a servant – on a donkey • People fell before him and worshipped him • "The whole world is going after him"

Appendix 5 – Memory Verses

❏ **1**   **New Life in Christ - 2 Corinthians 5:17**
Therefore, if anyone is in Christ, he is a new creation; the old
has gone, the new has come!

❏ **2**   **Fellowship Together - Hebrews 10:25**
"Let us not give up meeting together, as some are in the habit of
doing, but let us encourage one another–and all the more as
you see the Day approaching."

❏ **3**   **All Scripture - 2 Timothy 3:16-17**
"All Scripture is God-breathed and is useful for teaching, rebuk-
ing, correcting and training in righteousness, so that the man of
God may be thoroughly equipped for every good work"

❏ **4**   **God Answers Prayer - John 15:7**
"If you remain in me and my words remain in you, ask whatever
you wish, and it will be given you"

❏ **5**   **Obeying God's Word - James 1:22**
"Do not merely listen to the word, and so deceive yourselves.
Do what it says"

❏ **6**   **Eternal Life in Jesus - John 5:24**
"I tell you the truth, whoever hears my word and believes him
who sent me has eternal life and will not be condemned; he has
crossed over from death to life."

❏ **7**   **Jesus Forgives Me - 1 John 1:9**
"If we confess our sins, he is faithful and just and will forgive us
our sins and purify us from all unrighteousness"

❏ **8**   **God Loves Me - Psalms 103:11**
"For as high as the heavens are above the earth, so great is his
love for those who fear him"

❏ **9 God's Spirit Changes Me - Romans 8:9**

"You, however, are controlled not by the sinful nature but by the Spirit, if the Spirit of God lives in you. And if anyone does not have the Spirit of Christ, he does not belong to Christ"

❏ **10 Witnessing for Christ - 1 Peter 3:15**

"But in your hearts set apart Christ as Lord. Always be prepared to give an answer to everyone who asks you to give the reason for the hope that you have. But do this with gentleness and respect"

❏ **11 Living By Faith - Philippians 4:13**

"I can do everything through him who gives me strength"

❏ **12 Victory Over Sin - 1 Corinthians 10:13**

"No temptation has seized you except what is common to man. And God is faithful; he will not let you be tempted beyond what you can bear. But when you are tempted, he will also provide a way out so that you can stand up under it"

❏ **13 Let Your Light Shine - Matthew 5:16**

"... Let your light shine before men, that they may see your good deeds and praise your Father in heaven"

❏ **14 Forgiving Each Other - Ephesians 4:32**

"Be kind and compassionate to one another, forgiving each other, just as in Christ God forgave you"

❏ **15 The Cheerful Giver - 2 Corinthians 9:7**

"Each man should give what he has decided in his heart to give, not reluctantly or under compulsion, for God loves a cheerful giver"

Appendix 6 - Record Book of Sin

1	*Hold out both your hands*	These 2 hands represent hands 2 people.
2	*Now hold out just your right hand*	This hand represents the first person - me - *(give your name)*
3	*Place a book on your hand to represent sin*	But I have a problem - I sin against God. This book will represent a list of all my sins. My sin stops me from enjoying life with God. And God says my sin must be punished. So if I do nothing about my sin, and I stand before God to be judged - and he has to make a decision about whether I get into heaven, what will he say? Why? *(Wait for anwer, and help if needed)*
4	*Take away your right hand with the book, and hold out your left hand.*	This second hand represents Jesus. He never sinned. Never deserved any punishment from God at all. So if Jesus were to stand before God to be judged, and God had to make a decision as to whether he would get into heaven - what would God say? (Wait for anwer, and help if needed)
5	*Bring back your left hand with the book*	When Jesus dies on the cross- he takes the sin from all those who will turn and follow him ....

6  *Transfer the book from your right hand to your left*	... and places that sin on himself. He suffers the punishment - the hell - that I deserve for my sins.. The bible says **"All of us have gone astray; each one of us has turned to his own way, but God has laid on Jesus the sin of us all"** **(Isaiah 53:6)** So what does God see when he looks at Jesus dying on the cross ? (look at left hand with book - wait for answer) And whose sin? (wait for answer) So what does God now see when he looks at me? (look at left hand with book - wait for answer) So if I were to stand before God now - to be judged - and he had to decide whether I go to heaven, what would he say? Why? (look at left hand with book - wait for answer) And Jesus didn't stay dead - but rose from the grave and now rules with God his father!
7 *Put the book down, and pick it up again, so as not to confuse this with Jesus*	That means there are only 2 sorts of people in the world. Which one of these best represents where you are at right now?

Appendix 7 - Crossfire Ministry Training Curriculum

COURSE 0 PEER MINISTRY TRAINING	For all D-Team Students
1. Why Crossfire?	To understand the basic "Why" of Crossfire. Memorise the answers to the 3 questions
2. How to develop the HABITS of a disciple	To develop your personal walk with Jesus – so you have something to offer others
3. How to be a PEER Minister	To understand the 4 PEER steps: Pray, Encourage, Evangelise, Equip
4. How to share your faith	Introduction to "The Record Book of Sin" as a simple explanation of the gospel.
COURSE 1 INTRODUCTION TO CHRISTIAN LEADERSHIP	Level 1 Apprentices
1. Introduction to Crossfire	Refresher of Peer Ministry 1 Understanding the Vision of Crossfire
2. Introduction to Christian Leadership	The biblical qualities of a Christian leader
3. Introduction to Encouragement	Being positive. Speaking words of life. Being an encourager
4. Introduction to Leading Younger Kids	The "how to" of leading, inspiring, disciplining, directing …
COURSE 2 MINISTRY THAT CHANGES LIVES	Level 2 Apprentices
1. How to lead a small group	How to teach the bible in a small group; group dynamics; dealing with difficult students
2. How to help students personally	Introduction to pastoral care; Introduction to "counselling"; how to be an active listener

3. How to bring a student to Christ	How to minister to a student who responds to an challenge to take a step for Jesus
4. How to lead on a camp	How to be a cabin leader; small group leader's roles and responsibilities; discipline; the duty of care
COURSE 3 **A HEART FOR MINISTRY**	**Level 3 Apprentices**
1. The Heart of a Shepherd	"'Tend the flock of God that is your charge"; understanding the heart of Jesus; being a true shepherd
2. The Heart of a Servant	Understanding servanthood, followership, submission. Understanding the heart of Jesus
3. The Heart for Prayer	The ministry of prayer; the centrality of prayer; the passion for prayer
4. The Heart for Reliability	letting your "yes" mean "yes"; being available, being reliable; understanding commitment
COURSE 4 **STARTING OUT AS A** **YOUTH LEADER**	**First Year leaders**
1. The Biblical Basis for Youth Ministry	Understand from the bible what God has called us to do at Crossfire – therefore our purpose, mission, strategy.
2. My commitment as a Youth Leader	Understand the "high integrity" needed in a youth leader; understand what commitment means; introduction to the duty of care & legal implications
3. Turning Rebels to Worshippers	Refresher course on "How to bring a Student to Christ". How to give a credible explanation of the gospel, and invite students to respond. How to follow up and integrate

	Crossfire Leaders	D-Team Coaches
4. Starting in Leadership	Introduction to being a Crossfire leader. the roles of a CF leader; Being pro-active in leadership	How to run a D-Team. Keeping your team on track. Achieving biblical goals; growing disciples
5. Starting in Small Groups	How to lead a Discovering Jesus Group	How to teach and apply the bible in a small group
COURSE 5 DEVELOPING THE HEART OF JESUS	**2nd year + leaders**	
1. Being a New Testament Shepherd / pastor	The 3 relationships of a NT shepherd; the 3 tasks of a NT shepherd	
2. Developing the character of Jesus	Faithfulness, reliability, submission, excellence, perseverance, servanthood – developing character!	
3. Caring for individuals	The basic steps of counselling, listening, pastoral care, practical care	
4. Students in Crisis	Dealing with emotional trauma, abuse, divorce, suicide, bereavement	
COURSE 6 HOW TO BE A LEADER OF LEADERS	**Youth Key Leaders (Year Co-ordinators, Team Leaders, Jun/ Sen Hi pastors)**	
1. How to lead leaders	The difference between leading students and leading leaders. The basics of inspiring a team	
2. Being a positive encourager	How to build your team with words of life; how to be an active listener; how to encourage	
3. Developing and Correcting leaders	How to build leaders, develop their style. How to correct leaders without discouraging them	
4. Sowing a vision	How to establish and cast a vision before your leaders; how to work prayerfully towards a goal; being future oriented	